Explorations in Nar

STUDIES IN PROFESSIONAL LIFE AND WORK
Volume 6

Scope
The series will commission books in the broad area of professional life and work. This is a burgeoning area of study now in educational research with more and more books coming out on teachers' lives and work, on nurses' life and work, and on the whole interface between professional knowledge and professional lives.

The focus on life and work has been growing rapidly in the last two decades. There are a number of rationales for this. Firstly, there is a methodological impulse: many new studies are adopting a life history approach. The life history tradition aims to understand the interface between people's life and work and to explore the historical context and the socio-political circumstances in which people's professional life and work is located. The growth in life history studies demands a series of books which allow people to explore this methodological focus within the context of professional settings.

The second rationale for growth in this area is a huge range of restructuring initiatives taking place throughout the world. There is in fact a world movement to restructure education and health. In most forms this takes the introduction of more targets, tests and tables and increasing accountability and performativity regimes. These initiatives have been introduced at governmental level – in most cases without detailed consultation with the teaching and nursing workforces. As a result there is growing evidence of a clash between people's professional life and work missions and the restructuring initiatives which aim to transform these missions. One way of exploring this increasingly acute clash of values is through studies of professional life and work. Hence the European Commission, for instance, have begun to commission quite large studies of professional life and work focussing on teachers and nurses. One of these projects – the Professional Knowledge Network project has studied teachers' and nurses' life and work in seven countries. There will be a range of books coming out from this project and it is intended to commission the main books on nurses and on teachers for this series.

The series will begin with a number of works which aim to define and delineate the field of professional life and work. One of the first books 'Investigating the Teacher's Life and Work' by Ivor Goodson will attempt to bring together the methodological and substantive approaches in one book. This is something of a 'how to do' book in that it looks at how such studies can be undertaken as well as what kind of generic findings might be anticipated.

Future books in the series might expect to look at either the methodological approach of studying professional life and work or provide substantive findings from research projects which aim to investigate professional life and work particularly in education and health settings.

Explorations in Narrative Research

Edited by

Ivor F. Goodson, Avril M. Loveless and David Stephens

University of Brighton, Sussex, UK

SENSE PUBLISHERS
ROTTERDAM/BOSTON/TAIPEI

A C.I.P. record for this book is available from the Library of Congress.

ISBN: 978-94-6091-986-2 (paperback)
ISBN: 978-94-6091-987-9 (hardback)
ISBN: 978-94-6091-988-6 (e-book)

Published by: Sense Publishers,
P.O. Box 21858,
3001 AW Rotterdam,
The Netherlands
https://www.sensepublishers.com/

Printed on acid-free paper

TABLE OF CONTENTS

IVOR GOODSON, AVRIL LOVELESS AND DAVID STEPHENS

PREFACE

The genesis of this book—or perhaps back story—is a University of Brighton research grant awarded to the editors early in 2011. The grant was to support a number of initiatives related to the development of narrative research, particularly in the field of education. Since then the Education Research Centre at Brighton, where the three editors work—has seen the emergence of a strong interest in exploring new directions in narrative research.

Two major initiatives have been the establishment of an international network of narrative researchers and the holding of a symposium on 'narratives and learning'. This 'Narratives, Context and Learning' symposium took place on the 16–17th May 2011, hosted by the editors of this volume. Leading academics, some of whom have contributed to this book, came from Asia, Latin America, Northern Europe, Ireland and universities in the UK.

This book grows from this symposium not only in its content but also in the process by which contributions were presented, critiqued and finally published.

Participants to the symposium and subsequent contributors to this book were invited to discuss their own and each other's work in a collaborative and collegial manner. All discussion was transcribed and then offered to each contributor to this volume as a resource to use in the redrafting of the subsequent chapters.

As a result, though each chapter represents the particular interest of the author, it also reflects the wisdom and critique of the symposium members gathered together to explore new directions in narrative research.

What has emerged is a fascinating—and we hope useful—body of work generally exploring narrative enquiry and more specifically themes of culture and context, identity, teacher education, and methodology.

The symposium, this volume and the inauguration of an international network of narrative scholars are forming the basis of a future story we hope to tell.

We would like to take this opportunity to thank a number of people and our own institution who helped in the production of this book.

AFFILIATION

Ivor Goodson, Avril Loveless and David Stephens
University of Brighton

IVOR F. GOODSON

1. INVESTIGATING NARRATIVITY

An Introductory Talk by Ivor Goodson, Professor of Learning Theory,
University of Brighton

INTRODUCTION

In this chapter I have followed the format of the symposium on which the book is
based. We began with the following talk which tries to set the scene of some recent
investigations into the nature of narrativity. In this chapter we have chosen to stay
with the conversational tone to capture the kind of interactions which went on as
papers were delivered at the symposium. The talk has since formed a part of the
book called *Narrative Pedagogy* (Goodson and Gill, 2011) and will be further
developed in a forthcoming book, *Developing Narrative Theory* (Goodson, 2013).

SPENCER PROJECT 1998–2003

I shall be describing the kind of projects I have been involved in over the last ten or
so years to show how I have arrived at my understanding of how narratives
themselves get differentiated. Not a great deal of work has been done on how
narratives can be differentiated or asking the question, 'Are there different types of
narrative, different types of narrative character?' and I wanted to talk through how
I got to that place. I mean it started really with a project I was doing when I was in
North America (we talked about border crossings yesterday—well one of my more
problematic border crossings was when I was spending a bit of time in North
America after the miners' strike collapsed). I went there in 1985 and was there till
1996 and right up to 2000—in Rochester, New York.

The first project in which I became involved in narratives was during a project I
was doing with Andy Hargreaves, which was funded by the Spencer Foundation. It
was essentially looking at 'Education 2000', a Bill Clinton initiative—the purpose
was to find out why all the money they were spending—billions and billions of
dollars—was not emanating into any serious reforms in schools. They got so
desperate in the end that they started inviting quite radical theorists to come in and
help. We then sat around chatting and decided that the best way to understand how
and why educational reform processes were foundering was to conduct life history
interviews with a whole set of teachers in schools, together with life histories of the
schools themselves, to see how longitudinally, over time, reforms either succeeded
or did not succeed—were embedded or dis-embedded. So we started to collect
these very detailed life histories of teachers in a variety of schools in the New York
State and in Toronto and what we discovered was in itself really interesting. The

Ivor F. Goodson, Avril M. Loveless and David Stephens (Eds.), Explorations in Narrative Research, 1–10.
© *2012 Sense Publishers. All rights reserved.*

specific thing we discovered was that there was a clear spectrum (and this is no surprise in many ways), a clear spectrum of teachers—from those who complied fairly closely with any reform to those who developed a more personalised response. The first group accepted their role as technicians, following government guidelines... when a new script came they then followed this script just as obediently as they had followed the earlier script. This in essence is the history of the way teachers responded to neoliberal reforms in England. Many of them, probably more than any country in Europe have been compliant. Although we can talk about variations of resistance and decoupling, basically they have been complying. That is one end of the spectrum. The other end was a group of teachers who actually we could itemise... they were in some sense the best teachers. What they do in North America is that they give awards for the most creative teachers so you know pretty quickly who the elite, the vanguard of teachers—is. Now the vanguard of teachers were the more creative ones and if you talked to them about their life histories they had a very self-defined, quasi autonomous, 'elaborated' life history. They were in touch with their life history not in a 'scripted' way but in a partially self-defined way. Those people of course responded to reforms and scripts in a completely different way—though of course in the end many of them did give up, simply resign and retire in the face of being told that they had to become technicians following strict government guidelines.

DEVELOPING PERSPECTIVE: THREE STORIES

This had started me thinking about the different kinds of 'narrative character' and how that leads us to understand differentiated forms of social action and social response to particular social situations and curricular reforms. And then what always happens with me... I think it is because of what I said yesterday... I grew up in a family where everything was narrative but it was not a literate family... when I get a new idea it is very seldom from reading a book. It is more likely to be from a random conversation or something very concretely personal. I have learnt over time that if I have any ideas, that is where they come from. They don't come from some review of literature but rather, I tend to learn from a particular conversation I've had. And there are two conversations which after the Spencer project—we are talking 2003 now—which started to get me thinking about 'narrative capacities', 'narrative character', 'narrative elaborations'. The stories were these... and I have to mention my mum because I mentioned her yesterday (my mum died aged 104 last week and I am partly grieving and she comes into all my stories... anyhow...)-I was talking to her when she was 99... and to recap, she was 75 and she started to write poetry and that is how she defined herself—as a poet. And the main problem with her poetry was that it was absolutely dreadful! It was like, 'the cat shat on the mat!!!' kind of stuff. It was really a poor kind of poetry. And anyhow... when she was 99 she said, 'I've got a really interesting weekend, me duck. I am going to a poetry gathering in Torquay. They have a poet in residence and we are all going to gather round and give our poems, you see?' So I went down that weekend and said to her, 'How did the poetry weekend go?' She said, 'It wasn't good duck, it wasn't good at all. They all gave their poems—very elaborate poems... all sorts of complicated things that didn't rhyme properly and then I gave my poem and there was a terrible silence at the end of it and I said, "Oh!" And you wouldn't believe it, they invited all the people to come to the next poetry symposium and they didn't mention me'. So I said, trying to soften the blow to her sense of identity and aspiration, 'Mum I think it is just possible that you are not going to make it as a poet'. She was 99. She looked at me and said... there was a long pause... and she said, 'Yeah you could be right'. And I realised that this 99 year old woman was still in the process of aspiring and becoming and that was her narrative.

The second story is about somebody who colleagues here know—a Chinese guy called Rocky who I was in Beijing with, walking around... I had been talking all day and was fairly tired and he said, 'Let's have a walk round Beijing'. So we are walking around and after three hours I am tired and I said, 'Can we go and have a beer?' So we sit down and have a beer and he has a Coco-Cola and all that while he has been telling me the story of his life. I have been asking him his story and it is basically a fairly conventional Chinese cultural storyline of ancestors... what happened during the Mao period and so on... a fairly sequential, conventional story and I am struggling with his name which is Gaozheng and he said, 'Well you can call me Rocky?' And as we are having a Coke I said, 'Does Rocky have a different life story?' And he said, 'Oh yes'. And then he told me a completely western version of the life story.

What this hints at is that this spectrum of different narrativities means that people appropriate and work with domination, colonisation and individualisation in very different ways. So we have to... rather than assert that there are over-arching dominant western narratives that dominate everybody, we have to look at how different forms of narrativity respond, refract and generally re-interpret and redirect this domination. Domination is not a unilateral discourse. It is a discourse that is responded to, reiterated, reflected, refracted in different ways. And what I wanted to argue is that to understand people's narrative character and capacity is to understand how they appropriate and respond to discourses in different ways. A long time ago I wrote that domination is less about domination by dominant interest groups—more about solicitous surrender by subordinate groups. I always had this rather different view of domination.

THE PROFESSIONAL KNOWLEDGE PROJECT

When I moved to Brighton to work in 2003 more by luck than judgement I got funding for two very big projects. One was funded by the ESRC which was called the 'Learning Lives' project and one called the 'Professional Knowledge' project (the latter is a study of restructuring of seven European countries funded by the EU). And both funded by a million pounds... big projects and we have big research teams and we have to think hard about the methodology and in both cases we use a methodology that is broadly looking at life history. So let's take the 'Professional Knowledge' project first. This is a study of Finland, Sweden, Greece,

Portugal, Spain, Ireland and England—seven countries and it is looking at how teachers, nurses and doctors respond to restructuring... in each of those countries we are looking at a neoliberal world movement and how the different work-life narrative of teachers respond to it, are juxtaposed with what we call the 'systemic narratives', which are the rhetorics of reform. So what we are able to do there at a fairly simple national level way is show how a lot of... what we had there in terms of data is a range of quite detailed work life narratives from a range of teachers and doctors and nurses and we are showing the collision between different forms of narratives and reform initiatives—the systemic narratives. It was looking at how people's narrative character led to different responses to systemic reforms. So this was not some kind of arid discussion of narrative. It looked at how particular narrative predispositions often lead to particular political orientations and responses to systemic change and we... I could take you through the charts I have here but I won't because I want to stay with the narrative idea. Getting back to the 'Professional Knowledge' project—that was a high level attempt to understand how different work life narratives and different cultural narratives lead to very different national responses to systemic reform. So you take two examples... if you look at the spectrum of those seven countries—the most compliant country in terms of their implementation of neoliberalism was the British (very odd given our history). By far the most compliant of all the European countries in terms of neo-liberalism by a long way, while the most resistant to the reforms were the Finnish. Now interestingly to make a political point here—if you look at those two countries and then you look at the PISA Table of Performance—which I don't trust—you find the country that is most compliantly following neo-liberalism comes bottom of the league in performance and the country that has most resistant to it comes top. Now that should tell you that a lot of these neoliberal forms have very little to do with educational performance and everything to do with economic restructuring. I mean you don't have to be a brain surgeon to work out that this is an absurd situation—sorry to make a rather cheap party political point here—but it can't be ignored...

THE LEARNING LIVES PROJECT

Time is running out so let us move onto the second research project, the 'Learning Lives' project. This is the one where so much of the kinds of theorising came up. We were given four years and the basic... I'd better fill in the gaps... what it was, was the New Labour project called 'The Teaching and Learning Program'... this had three phases and was funded by the Economic and Social Research Council. What we really wanted to do was find ways of reconceptualising teaching and learning. That was the stated aspiration and we came in with a quite large bid. It was based on four universities: Leeds, Exeter, Brighton and Stirling and it was going to look at how people learnt throughout the life course—particularly interested in lifelong learning and particularly interested in the kinds of transitional moments of people's learning. And what we wanted to do was to talk to a cluster of ordinary folk—if you can put it that way—who talked to us about their lives.

When I say in detail... we were doing three-hour interviews, often eight times with each person... so we are talking seriously detailed life history stuff. And we had a big team of people across the universities. I think at different times we had about 18 people working on this and our particular set of tasks here in Brighton was to look at migrant groups. So we looked at a group of people, from asylum seekers through to a more privileged set of migrants, through to homeless people, through to a wide range of working people, farmers and others. We had members of the House of Lords. We had some very famous creative artists. We had a pretty interesting bunch of people of all sorts and the first thing that came clear, and I think this is a reminder that cultural storylines do not monolithically impinge on social groups... if you were to characterise their different social character... there were just as many people of 'one kind' at one end of the social spectrum as at the other. You had just as many 'elaborated life stories' among working groups as you did among members of the House of Lords. It wasn't in that sense socially stratified, rather a random scatter of different narrativities. And I would say that there was a random scatter of narrativities across cultures as well. Our initial finding was that once again, the spectrum of 'scripted' versus 'elaborated' narratives emerged. One type of narrative was what we called the 'describers'. Describers tend to describe what has happened to them in a kind of... this was who I was, this is what I am... I was a housewife, I was a farmer, kind of way... it is a kind of acceptance of a birthright script that society assigned to them and they work with that script, and when they talk about their life story they describe it in a kind of retrospective description of what had happened to them. In other words it is less active. It is a description rather than what I called an 'elaboration'. 'Elaborators' are ones who... I mean who would be a quintessential elaborator? Obama would be one. Bill Clinton would be one. Those kinds of people in a sense invented a persona then they became it. You know—one of our key informants was a guy who had grown up with two alcoholic parents and had basically decided aged seven he would become the best puppeteer in England and that was his script from very early on and that is indeed was what he became. He kind of defined a narrative for himself and then in a sense inhabited it. He became it. He kind of self-defined himself, in a sense, using all the scripts that are out there. This was not a complete act of self-invention, it was in a sense an act of 'collage'. It was an act of mosaic. It was an act of creating a coat of many colours which is you. So there you have 'description' and 'elaboration'.

With this project what I was trying to work out was the relationship between narrativity and what I call 'courses of action'. The project was called 'Learning Lives, Identity, Agency and Learning' and we were looking at the relationship between 'agency and learning'. How do these descriptions of 'narrative character' emanate in the delineation of 'courses of action'? How do we become active in the world? How do we put our imprint on the world? My initial assumption seems commonsensically sustainable... it was that the 'describers', since they seem to have passively accepted a script, would not be practiced in a 'course of action'. They would be more passive. And the 'elaborators' because they are active in the construction of their narrative would be more active in the world. Strangely that proved to both true and false because as you see when I... let me show me this table... (see TABLE 1)

TABLE 1
NARRATIVITY, AGENCY AND KNOWLEDGE

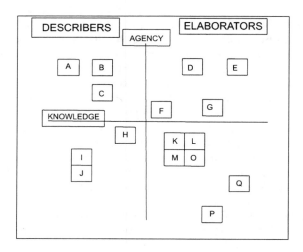

...as you see here this is a relationship between knowledge and agency—knowledge being in a sense 'narrative knowledge'. Far from there being a monolithic relationship between knowledge and agency it falls into four different clusters.

What I began to realise as we revealed people's narrative lives was that there was a spectrum—from those people who essentially described their lives as something that had happened to them—to others who elaborated their own story, drawing on a range of storylines and cultural resources to develop their own personal 'mosaic'.

But the distinction between 'describers' and 'elaborators' was only the beginning of our analysis. Once you analyse people's actions in the world their capacity to delineate courses of action—the narrative map becomes more complex.

Looking at the chart—on the left you have 'describers'. In the top left you have 'describers'. They normally accepted a role early in life—a kind of 'birthright script'—be it a farmer or hairdresser or policewoman—and stuck with it. Whilst the script worked they were fine but because they were unpractised in defining their own courses of action sharp transitions often left them in difficulty. Their main commitment was to an ascribed role and their learning stayed close to that role. We came to see this group as 'scripted describers'.

But commitment to a script did not always mean a limitation of agency. Other people, in the bottom left of the chart, whilst embracing a script nonetheless often moved from script to script, even from country to country. We called this group 'multiple describers'. Their learning was most often focussed on their life role but as they changed scripts so they flexibly embraced new learning strategies. We studied a number of migrants who whilst primarily 'describers' of their life had embraced new scripts and new challenges throughout their lives.

On the right hand side 'elaborators' were similarly complex when their agency was analysed. In the right bottom corner were what we called 'focussed elaborators'. These people seem to spend a good deal of time working on their narrative and linking it to their activities. Often a narrative of aspiration led onto a life vocation. An example would be Barack Obama—who has written eloquently about his developing life narratives and his hopes and dreams. This narrative facility provides him with huge 'narrative capital' for the task of developing political narratives for his country. Bill Clinton is similar in his elaborative facility.

In case you're wondering, David Cameron seems to me the opposite—born into a birthright script he has had little practice in elaboration. Whilst he has high 'cultural capital' he has low 'narrative capital'. No wonder people find it hard to know what he's trying to do. His one attempt 'The Big Society' provided definitive evidence of this lack of narrative facility. This reminds me of Sylvia Plath's mother's complaint to Ted Hughes, sitting in her privileged affluent home where Sylvia grew up. She complains to Ted, 'Well she never had your advantages'. Son of the proletariat Hughes asks, 'And what might they be?' She replies, 'The need to fight for everything you've got and to know its value'. Hughes likewise knew how to command and elaborate a narrative storyline.

The capacity to link an elaborated storyline to a course of action means these narrators can respond flexibly to new situations. They are practiced in what I call 're-selfing' and continuous learning.

However not all elaborators are like this. Some are brilliant at developing narratives—seem almost to live 'in narration'. They talk at length, and lucidly, about their views and dreams and experiences. But for some this is not successfully linked to the development of 'courses of action'. We call them therefore 'armchair elaborators'. Their learning likewise is not related to new courses of action of the development of new identity projects. Their learning is often instrumental, often linked to other peoples' plans from whom paradoxically autonomy is sought. Armchair elaborators find transitions difficult and their narratives have a somewhat circular character—often revolving around some initial obstacle or trauma.

The key thing for me is... what I am writing about at the moment is... if you think about the seismic changes and shifts in the world at the moment and all of that stuff about flexible labour forces and flexible manpower and flexible accumulation... one of the key things I am interested in is 'flexibility of response' to situations. But I talk about that as a capacity for 're-selfing'. As conditions change you get a flexible response for 're-selfing' (I call that 're-selfing'). We were talking earlier Molly, about where self-belief comes from. We were saying, and both of us agree, that partly, self-belief is related to people's 'narrative'

7

capacity. In other words—the capacity to delineate paths of action which they believe in and then making those 'courses of action' happen. When that happens you build up your self-belief and part of that is your capacity to respond flexibly to new situations and to find a new narrative and a new form of self that represents the passage within. It relates to learning styles... and remember that this was a project about learning as well as narrativity. So if you go through some of the things here... for me, learning... what constitutes learning? Is it something defined by somebody else that you take into yourself and then it is learnt? That is the cognitive model of learning. What I am wanting to put in my narrative book is that learning... there is another form of learning which I would call learning where there are substantial shifts in the self. When the self shifts the sense of the self shifts—that is learning as a primal epicentral kind... so behind the debate here is... what constitutes learning? And I think there is the most interesting work going on here at our research centre on narratives. In different ways Avril, David... everybody... Tim certainly is... looking at how one re-conceptualises learning styles? How do we reconceptualise a learning theory to come up with a more conclusive modality for learning? So there is this whole debate behind this about what constitutes learning... when you start looking at narrativity you start to embrace the notion that the process of becoming somebody and the process of re-selfing is in itself learning. I mean commonsensically learning is more than learning a few bits of Latin and a few bits of history... isn't it a finding of a way to shift your whole narrative self?

There are other ways I think that having this more differentiated view of narratives helps us. I mean think about professional development... if we, instead of assuming that people are monolithically similar in terms of their narrative capacity, if we have a more differentiated view of professional teaching development and learning, it is much more likely it will be targeted in a more personalised way. So there is an argument for a much more distinctive, a much more person-centred education than the conventional notion of education which is cognitive and which assumes a kind of homogenised sense of the learning audience. I think we can examine the many implications of differentiation... in terms of political activism, in terms of political orientation... in the way whole nation states respond differently (to go back to Carl Anders thing and the different notions of nationhood). All of these things... but that is enough from me! I've said enough and time is ticking on... I'm looking forward to what you all have to say... so I'll stop here!

REFERENCES

Economic and Social Research Council (ESRC) (2003–2008). Learning lives: learning, identity and agency in the life course. ESRC Teaching & Learning Research Programme. University of Brighton, University of Exeter, University of Stirling, University of Leeds. http://www.learninglives.org/index.html

European Union (2002–2008) 'Professional knowledge in education and health (PROFKNOW): restructuring work and life between state and citizens in Europe. University of Brighton, University of Gothenburg, National and Kopodistorian University of Athens, University of Joensuu, University of Barcelona, University of the Azores, St. Patrick's College Dublin City University, University of Stockholm. http://www.ips.gu.se/english/Research/research_programmes/pop/current_research/profknow/

Goodson, I. F. (2013). *Developing narrative theory*. London: Routledge.

Goodson, I. F., & Gill, S. (2011). *Narrative pedagogy*. New York: Peter Lang.

Goodson I. F., & Hargreaves, A. (1998–2003). 'Change over time? A study of culture, structure, time and change in secondary schooling'. USA: The Spencer Foundation.

AFFILIATION

Ivor Goodson
Education Research Centre,
University of Brighton

CARL ANDERS SÄFSTRÖM

2. URGENTLY IN NEED OF A DIFFERENT STORY

Questioning Totalising Frameworks

A question is by definition something that comes before an answer. If it is not, it is rather, a proposition. All knowledge starts from a question bordering on unknown territory. If that territory is already known the case is, so to speak, closed. To paraphrase Richard Rorty (1980) science has through history tried to close the case, to find the final truth. Every such attempt, though, has later been proved to be wrong. Two things follow from this. First, if the moment comes when there is a final truth, it would be awfully quiet thereafter; all would be said and done, all communication coming to a halt. Secondly, what researchers need, is not yet another truth. What they need, is therapy in order to be able to live with contingency. I think that in addition to it, the researcher needs to look into his or her preconceptions of things while exploring others. So in exploring the shortcomings of totalising frameworks in what follows, I start with questioning one of my own—my nationality.

Nationality is never so important as when one is crossing borders. At the border it is decided who can enter and who cannot. But also, entering that 'passage' turns you from being self-evidently 'in your nationality' into a stranger. Yet, in addition to becoming a stranger, the passage itself opens the possibility to perceive one's nationality from within and from without simultaneously—it creates a space for reflection. In the first section of this chapter I recount a memory of a story that made me reflect on national identity. It is a story of an experience/memory in which what 'being Swedish' means is seriously challenged. I tell this here in order to discuss the limits imposed on education by totalising frameworks, such as national identity. I discuss how these frameworks limit the very possibility of a democratic citizenship. Even though I specifically use Sweden as an example I'm not arguing that Sweden is a special case, it just happens that I'm Swedish, which means whatever that means—it is in 'my soul and bones'. Therefore, reflecting on being Swedish means that I cannot stand entirely outside that experience but am somewhat also in it—there is no outside, I'm included by definition. Just as (good) humour is a way of creating cracks in the surface of living—narratives and narrative research can be an effective way of exposing that surface and making it visible for in-depth analysis (see also Gill & Goodson, 2011). That is what I'm doing in this chapter, through my story, I'm exploring the limits of a totalising frame, regardless of if that frame is being imposed by others or not, or being held to be a truth in my life. That is to say, it is the 'figure' of nationalism as a totalising framework—that is my target to expose, since it takes away the possibility of politics and the possibility of having another idea, another worldview, another life

Ivor F. Goodson, Avril M. Loveless and David Stephens (Eds.), Explorations in Narrative Research, 11–20.

other than the one prepared for you, by birth, by culture, by context, by school and society. There is no other possibility within a totality, just variations within the same framework. Once I have told my story and distanced myself from it by treating it as a conceptual story for analysis I move on to a conceptual context in which totalising frameworks are deconstructed.

In the second section I identify what I will call the story of 'one', the idea that societies develop and grow organically, that they are natural expressions of certain characteristics, that all those who are 'counted in' belong to—share in. I also introduce a distinction between distributive politics and the political, in line with Chantal Mouffe (2005). This distinction is introduced so as to pinpoint a fundamental division in society, beyond the story of 'one', between those who have access to power and wealth and those who have not. I also in this section demonstrate how political discourse is turned into moral discourse, again taking Sweden as example, and discussing some of the consequences of such a discourse.

In the third section I draw on Jacques Rancière's (1999) critique of the unequal society as being upheld by a political fiction, in order to specify the terms in which society is divided. I suggest that citizenship, insofar as it is a product of the idea of 'one', is basically apolitical and that schooling ends up preparing for such citizenship through a curriculum that emphasises national identity as an impossible framework for democracy and democratic citizenship. Curriculum is one of those useful plastic concepts which I take for meaning both the actual national curriculum of Sweden, but also a concept any school in any society has and which confirms the reality of that society, large or small in which schooling takes place. It confirms a reality already in place (see also Goodson, 1988).

In a concluding section I summarise my attempt to re-politicise the story of society beyond the totalising one of national identity and highlight some of the moves that need to be made in order to tell another story of education and democratic citizenship.

A STORY OF QUESTIONING NATIONAL IDENTITY

I'm sitting on a plane to Canada. It is my very first visit to that country. I'm nervous. It is not flying that makes me tense, though. I have been flying more times than I can remember. But what makes this flight different is that for the first time I am going to meet my beloved one in her country—a country I have little knowledge of. The plane is an ordinary Boeing operated by Air Canada. The service onboard is relaxed and very friendly. On the usual in-flight movie screen there is a film about Canada, of the sort where everything seems to glow if in an early morning mist or painted in red by a sunset. The film is about Niagara Falls, about ice wine, about hockey, about the CN tower in Toronto, the beauty of Vancouver which encapsulates the grandness of sea and mountains, and about the cultural mix of Montreal shown through its languages, architecture and public life. Since this is my first Air Canada flight I do watch with interest, and there is not much else to do anyway as I am too tired to read or write. The film is instructive, though, in telling me how the country wants to picture itself in ideal terms. Near the end of the film a narrator talks about what it means to be a

Canadian, a citizen of a country neighbouring the USA and which got its flag as late as 1965 and which just twenty years later reclaimed its constitution from the Queen of England and which has two official languages, French and English. 'To be Canadian is foremost to ask oneself just one question—what does it mean to be Canadian?' Isn't that just great! The very foundation of national identity is a question and not an already defined answer, even in a very polished PR film. Coming from the 'old world' this is simply astonishing. The very definition of nation states in Europe, seem on the contrary to be claiming to have an answer to precisely this sort of question. Or perhaps it is rather that the question does not really exist at all among the nation states since the answer is too self-evidently rooted in our minds and souls that people tend to believe, in the strongest sense of that word, that what they are is what the nation is. Presenting the nation in question is to present who they are. That this is the case is quite clear for me, particularly after a teaching incident with a group of student teachers. I gave a lecture discussing national identity by asking students to name so-called national characteristics. What we came up with was, of course, just superficial things such as: midsummer, snuff, certain types of food etc... and general things that can hardly be attached just to Swedes but rather are characteristics of humankind in general. Near the end of the lecture one young woman exploded, actually screaming on the top of her voice, 'Everybody knows what being Swedish means!!!!' The anxiety the question provoked was palpable in the room. To ask, 'What does it mean to be Swedish?' is clearly not the foundation of what being Swedish means. Posing the question produces anxiety, not only about one's identity as defined by nationhood, but about who you are, in a deep existential sense. For if being Swedish had no fundamental meaning for the young woman then her existence seemed to have no fundamental meaning, and who can live with that?

Landing in Canada went smoothly. The airport looked in some respects like all other airports in the world. If there is an identity of airports, they seem to share it. Lining up to show my passport and landing card my anxiety swept over me again. In my excited state I had marked not the usual 'business' but 'private' for my reasons for entering the country. The border official asked me my reasons for visiting the country, and I said, in my nervous state (severely increased by the sharp look from the officer) that I was there to meet my girlfriend (said with a certain pride). Well, the officer was not impressed. He stamped my card with what looked like a red big F (I always wondered if that meant Failure!) and sent me over to immigration. There was a row of chairs in front of some serious looking immigration officers. In the room, except for the officers, was me and two other unfortunate people from somewhere else in the world. I sat down where I was directed to sit (I tell you, there is no fooling around in an immigration office!). The immigration officer started to question me right away. 'What was the nature of my visit? How long did I intend to stay? What was my work?' And a series of other standard questions for an immigrant suspect. My nervousness started to vanish and instead there was a growing irritation on my part. After being harshly questioned for maybe ten minutes I had had it. I said strongly and with a great sense of indignation, without thinking what the consequences could be: 'I have come from Sweden, why on earth do you think I would want to stay in Canada?'

A remarkable thing happened, I was not sent to jail, or taken into a dark room to be beaten to a pulp or sent back to Sweden. The officer seemed to think; 'He is right, why on earth would he want to stay in Canada if he is from Sweden?' I was let off the hook and could go and pick up my bags and finally enter into Canada.

So what do I take from this story? Clearly immigration works differently for different people. Coming from the 'old world' to the 'new world' and from a country with a reputation of having an ideal welfare state can be handy in certain circumstances. The other two people in the immigration office were not, as far as I could see, let off the hook so easily and they didn't seem to come from Sweden. But who knows? What is clear is that the word 'Sweden' was a key for opening up the professional doubt of the immigration officer. 'Sweden' is a country you don't migrate from. It is as simple as that and as complicated.

National identity in nation states such as Sweden seems to be strongly and deeply rooted in the very sensible formation of meaningful lives. National identity cannot be reduced to a pose or something you choose, or something you learn in schools—rather it seems, comparable to the very air one breathes. Being Swedish is, in its fullest sense— 'one' identity—as I realised with the immigration office at Pearson Airport. It is an identity you are supposed to share with all the other people living in that space called Sweden, without asking the fundamental question of how that even is possible—and what being Swedish means?

Being Swedish should be understood in terms of a story one has to believe in, in order for it to be meaningful at all. How can such an abstract conception of being Swedish be anything else other than a fiction, even though this fiction has real consequences for many people? Society, in the words of Castoriadis (1987), is an imaginary concept, upheld by institutions, like immigration offices, and in this case when they are marking its borders. National identity as an expression of a particular society is therefore a fantasy, but a fantasy one holds as a life. The nature of such an identity is to be shared, it has to be recognised as the same identity of each and every one.

National identity is in the final analysis though, dependent on the idea of 'one', not many. Being Swedish means one thing, and that thing is reproduced through generations as a story. It is a story simply because there cannot be a 'thing' that all Swedes share, no molecule that distinguish someone as being Swedish—no gene. To be Swedish then is to be *in* the story, to love it as the truth of one's life. This story though, seems to be a story with no beginning or end, no clear characteristics making it unique in relation to other types of stories defining other national identities. The girl in my class was screaming, but inarticulate. The anxiety seemed to be based on the sudden insight that she was not able, in any clear cut way, to pin down what being Swedish could possibly mean, other than a superficial thing. It became rather a fundamental question of <u>Being</u> (Swedish) or <u>Being Nothing</u> (at all), to paraphrase Heidegger.

In relation to the Canadian experience it became clear to me that the story of being Swedish is an answer to an old and forgotten question: What is Swedishness? National identity is an answer to a forgotten question and it makes it impossible to really enter into that 'story' from the outside because it is beyond something one can learn or know in a rational way. National identity becomes more of a moral obligation without a rule defining it (and therefore essentially irrational). Canada has its own problems, of course (as was demonstrated at the airport) but asking the question so openly of who you are as a Canadian invites people to give different answers. The idea of a country is not the only one possibility but also many others. In Sweden, as an outsider you are always a 'failure' since you are not born into the nation story, but in Canada you are asked to contribute to the meaning of such a story.

THE IDEA OF 'ONE' AND MORAL POLITICAL DISCOURSE

As far as schooling is aimed at incorporating the young into being a certain type of citizen, different modes of being in a country's framework moulds citizenship differently. A Swedish national curriculum educates the young within a framework of national identity as being essentially 'one'. It is the idea of one organically developed society, of society as *Ochlos*, indivisible and total in its enclosure of everyone in its totality. Every Swede is what he or she is, against the backdrop of an idea of a totality in which everyone has his or her place. Individualism itself is to be understood in relation to such an idea. That is to say, the individual 'identities' are already defined within an idea of 'one'. This totality is the story that frames the national curriculum because curriculum is first and foremost an expression of the society's image, of how it understands itself. It defines the space and the story occupying that space. The national curriculum ensures that national Swedes are made and reproduced. It is an expression of how the state will ensure its own continuation (Popkewitz, 2008).

In curriculum this is called the basic or central value that has to be transmitted to each and everyone: 'The school has the important task of imparting, instilling and forming in pupils those fundamental values on which our society is based' (Lpo94, 2006, p. 1). Schooling then, as a fulfilment of curriculum, is a confirmation of an already on-going socialisation of living in the story that is Sweden. Schooling does not create national identity—schooling confirms what is already the case. One is born *in* the story. Therefore Swedish schools are for Swedish children, like British schools are for Brits or German schools for Germans. Immigrants are by definition outside of that story, and consequently experience systematic exclusion (Skolverket, [Board of Education], 1997). In Sweden this is most apparent in the language itself. You are labelled an immigrant even if you are born in Sweden a third generation immigrant (see Further Säfström, 2011).

My point here is that totality is one of inequality, but it is an inequality that is contained within a framework. In Rancière's (1999) words, the poor are included and excluded. That is, each and everyone is supposed to have his or her place within this framework which is unequally distributed in terms of power and wealth. Because this basic social inequality is distributed against the backdrop of the idea of 'one' there is no position from which politics can appear. Politics can only happen when *ochlos* is divided, when there are antagonisms between positions that are absolutely different to each other and where there is not a common frame neutralising them (Rancière, 1999; Mouffe, 2005). Such a framework reduces antagonisms to variations of a theme that has already been given meaning within the framework. It becomes fundamentally apolitical. That means, amongst other, things that if the idea of schooling is defined by a national curriculum, neutralising the possibility of antagonisms between different 'hegemonies'—democracy cannot be contained within such a framework. Democracy can only happen when the idea of a totality of society as *ochlos*, is divided. Therefore there are no democratic schools in Sweden, even though democracy can happen within them.

Using Chantal Mouffes' (2005) distinction between politics as distribution on one hand and the political on the other, as a confrontation of antagonisms on the other, one can say that in order for democratic citizenship to be political it needs to be divided. That is, it is only when distributive politics (to give each and everyone what he or she 'deserves' in the unequal organised society) is confronted with the antagonism of the political that it can really be democratic. It is only when one acknowledges that positions are not variations of the same theme but represent profoundly different world views, that the political can exist as such, that a political democracy can exist at all. For Mouffe, it is a question of transforming antagonisms into what she calls 'agonisms', that define 'the core' of a democratic citizenship. This agonism emerges when adversaries are acknowledged, when there is space for legitimate antagonisms rather than some kind of neutralising framework as, for example, national identity is.

If being Swedish can be understood in term of a moral obligation of being *in* the story, as suggested above, it is a story in which the inside is understood in terms of a fundamentally good story against the outside evils (Mattlar, 2008; Säfström, 2011). In a study of textbooks for teaching newly arrived immigrants and high school students the subject 'Swedish as a second language', Mattlar (2008) shows, how the evil coming from 'the outside' is characterised in terms of dictatorship/oppression, socio-economical segregation/misery, conflict/war, oppression of women, irrationality/chaos etc. Foreign societies are sharply distinguished from the good Swedish society in the same textbooks, as the latter is described as democratic, equal, peaceful, rational etc.

This means that what would be in a well-functioning democracy a legitimate political adversary is instead in the moral society reduced to an evil enemy which is in need of being dealt with in special way, so as not to contaminate the one good society itself. The one which in a proper democracy would be a legitimate adversary acting on the basis of a different hegemony becomes instead an absolute enemy whose legitimacy is not only seriously questioned but is turned into an evil threat to humanity itself. The moral political discourse dehumanises its enemies and therefore carries with it the seed for violent reactions that threatens to destroy political institutions. But the threat to political institutions is not only, for Mouffe (2005) coming from the outside but also from within. That is to say, political institutions can less and less account for and guarantee antagonistic political relations. Schooling is a paradigmatic example of that. In Sweden this is most apparent in the transformation of class conflicts, ethnic conflicts and gender conflicts into a question of discipline and order in schools (Månsson and Säfström, 2010). The ordered school is one in which the teacher is supposed to be the strong leader who moulds the students into 'good' citizens—that is, citizens that accept their given place within the story of the moral 'one'. And in as far as society and schooling reflect each other, what we are moving towards is a society in which the poor are as included as they are excluded. They are questioned on moral grounds as to whether they have the right to be supported by the state at all—as if they are enemies of the good (rich) citizen. So I do think we need to start to ask ourselves 'What does it mean to be Swedish?' or 'what does it mean to be English, or German?' or a member of any strongly defined nation in Europe. What I realised when confronted by the Canadian experience was that I do not know the country I live in just because I'm living in it. To know that, one would need to find a position outside the given story that presents itself as 'nature' rather than 'culture'.

THE POLITICAL FICTION CHALLENGED

The story of the 'one' establishes itself as a political fiction, which neutralises the political and turns democracy into the domain of rhetoric. The political fiction establishes itself as a rhetoric at war, rather than a reasoning one, according to Rancière. In rhetoric, one is not searching for real understanding—its sole aim is to take over the will of another person. Rhetoric is speech that revolts against the poetic condition for the speaking being—it is speech to silence someone else: 'You will speak no longer, you will think no longer, you will do this—that is its program' (Rancière 1991, p. 85). And it is only by being taken over by such a program that one becomes a part of the apolitical fiction of being a citizen in a post-political state as opposed to being a political subject. Or as Rancière (1991) formulates it:

> We aren't saying that the citizen is the ideal man, the inhabitant of an egalitarian political heaven that masks the reality of the inequality between concrete individuals. We are saying the opposite: that there is no equality except between men, that is to say, between individuals who regard each other only as reasonable beings. The citizen, on the contrary, the inhabitant of the political fiction, is man fallen into the land of inequality (ibid, p. 90).

Apolitical citizenship is foremost the result of a political fiction which from 'time immemorial' has been an expression of a passion for inequality (Rancière, 1991) — through what he calls a reciprocal subjugation: a subjugation, which has alienated the power from the people as the people have been alienated from the power. 'This reciprocal subjugation is the very principle of the political fiction whose origin lies in the alienation of reason by the passion of inequality' (ibid, p. 90).

Citizenship within the framework of national identity is also irrational because it tends to be based on a moral obligation without a rule. It is also unreasonable because it takes the political away from the subject and throws him or her into the land of inequality. For Ranciére it is human beings that can be equal, not social structures. And it is social structure that defines the nature of citizenship. What I have been arguing is that this social structure is based in the idea of 'one'. Being a citizen is neutralised by a story of nationhood and a moral obligation to be within that story or forever doomed outside the sphere of the good citizen. What is urgently needed is a story that it re-politicises not only democracy but also what it means to be living in a divided society, which turns the rich into the good citizen and the poor into bad ones.

The poor, says Rancière, are both included at the same time—nothing. The poor are included as part of 'the people' and have as much freedom as anyone else but they can in no way possess it. Therefore the poor are 'the part who has no part', the part, which is included in the whole but count for nothing. Rancière (1999) says '… through the existence of this part who have no part, of this nothing that is all, the community exists as a political community—divided by a fundamental dispute' (ibid p. 9). The political is a fundamental dispute over the division between those who have and those who do not have access to power and wealth. This fundamental division Rancière (1999) calls 'wrong' and becoming a political subject means challenging this wrong with claims for equality. When the singular being claims its right to speak, to be heard as much as anyone else, it also attaches itself to 'the conflict between the parties in society'. (ibid, p. 39)

By asserting the singular, universal 'wrong' the subject appears in democratic politics emancipated from the supposed naturalness of an unequal social order brings to the fore an essential conflict, namely, 'the very existence of something in common between those who have a part and those who have none' (ibid, p. 35).

Such subjectification, according to Rancière (1999) leads to a basic 'reconfiguration of the field of experience' (ibid, p. 35). Specifically it leads to a reconfiguration of the story of 'one', in my view, in such a way as to seriously question identification with national identity as a natural order, defining society in its totality. Political subjectification is a 'dis-identification', a removal from a place given to the subject and defined through national identity in the supposedly natural order of society. Instead it leads to an 'opening up of a subject space where anyone can be counted since it is the space where those of no account are counted' (ibid, p. 36). In other words in order to appear as a political subject, to be counted in, one needs to separate oneself from the story of national identity—a story which is nothing other than a expression of a neutralisation of an unequal society of rich and poor. And from this position one should ask, not what being Swedish means, but what living in a democratic society means? Such a question has to be asked openly.

CONCLUSION

In this chapter I have told a story which made me reflect upon what being Swedish could possibly mean, not just for me, but for others—as was reflected back to me by the point of view of the young woman screaming in my class or the immigration officer at Pearson airport, for example. I have suggested that being Swedish can be understood as an answer to an old and forgotten question, making citizenship apolitical to its core. Apolitical citizenship is both a condition of and a framework for the idea of schooling, as it appears in the national curriculum. That is, insofar as schooling is a reflection of a certain society, it carries with it the founding ideas of that society. The founding values of the Swedish curriculum refer to *the*

Swedish national identity as a story of 'one', which neutralises the unequal society of the rich and poor. In order for the political to take place at all, I have claimed that there is a need to divide the idea of society as a story of 'one', and to acknowledge different stories as not simply being variations of a common theme, but as representing radically different world views. It is also here that we can start to talk about the beginning of a different story, a story of politics proper. What instead takes place, as I have shown above is, by taking Sweden as an example, a moral discourse defines what is good and evil on the political stage—it discourages any possibility of legitimate confrontation of different world views. That means that in order for democracy to deal with multiple world views, to be at all possible in school and society, we urgently need a different story other than the one based on national identity that is a totalising framework that deprives the other of its otherness. Or differently put, what we need, I think, is to revitalise the art of asking questions about how to live with others in a way that does not deprive the very otherness of that other, regardless of how he or she supposedly differs from me. Totalising frameworks are contexts that suck the air out of any culture and, to return to the beginning, close the case for good—our task, as educationalists then is to throw any finality back to its contingent state of origin.

REFERENCES

Castoriadis, C. (1987). *The imaginary institution of society*. Cambridge, Massachusetts: The MIT Press.
Gill, S., & Goodson, I. (2011). *Narrative pedagogy: Learning from life history*. New York: Peter Lang.
Goodson, I. (1988). *The making of curriculum: Collected essays*. London: Falmer.
Lpo94 (2006). *Curriculum for the compulsory school system: The pre-school class and the leisure-time centre*. Stockholm: Fritzes.
Månsson, N. & Säfström, C. A. (2010). Tema: *Ordningens pris*. [Special issue: The Cost of Order]. *Utbildning & Demokrati, 19*(3).
Mattlar, J. (2008). Skolbokspropaganda? En ideologianalys av läroböcker I svenska som andraspråk (1995–2005). [Textbook propaganda? An ideology analysis of textbooks in Swedish as a second language 1995–2005]. Uppsala University. Studia Didactica Upsaliensia 1.
Mouffe, C. (2005). *On the political*. London: Routledge.
Popkewitz, T. (2008). *Cosmopolitanism and the age of school reform. Science, education, and making society by making the child*. London: Routledge.
Rancière, J. (1991). *The ignorant schoolmaster. Five lessons in intellectual emancipation*. Stanford, California: Stanford University Press.
Rancière, J. (1999). *Disagreement. Politics and philosophy*. Minneapolis: University of Minnesota Press.
Rorty, R. (1980). *Philosophy and the mirror of nature*. Oxford: Blackwell.
Säfström, C. A. (2011). The immigrant has no proper name: The disease of consensual democracy within the myth of schooling. In, special Issue: Rancière, Public Education and the Taming of democracy. *Educational Philosophy and Theory, 42*(5/6).
Skolverket, [Board of Education] (1997). *Barn mellan arv och framtid: Konfessionella, etniska och språkligt inriktade skolor I ett segregationsperspektiv*. Stockholm: Skolverket.

AFFILIATION

Carl Anders Säfström,
School of Education, Culture and Communication,
Mälardalen University, Sweden

RAGNA ÅDLANDSVIK

3. NARRATIVES AND OLD AGE

Stories were like blood running through a body—paths of a life

Siri Hustvedt

THE STORY STARTS

My contribution is a narrative about PEP, a personal and professional story about old age and verbal creativity. The PEP (*Prosjekt Eldrepedagogikk*) was a cooperative project between the County Library of Hordaland and University of Bergen, where my field was teacher education, in the years 1999–2003 and with follow ups in the years after. Creative writing and storytelling for elderly people was at the heart of the project (Ådlandsvik, 2007; Synnes, Saetre and Ådlandsvik, 2003).

PEP had five initial courses: three courses for people living at home, two for people in institutions, and one for people beginning to develop dementia. In this pilot we had around 45 participants between the ages of 67 and 90. They had widely varied professional backgrounds and came from both rural and urban areas. We met every second week over a period of one year.

Much of the inspiration came from my personal history as a school teacher and textbook writer of Norwegian language and literature for teenagers. I had seen so many magic moments where the creative potential of young people resulted in strikingly creative products through remarkable learning processes. Doors could be opened if the teacher found the right keys. Why shouldn't the same thing apply to old people?

We had a growing feeling that the oldest generations were marginalised, undervalued, and not 'included' in many aspects of our modern society. They were, in many cases culturally 'invisible'. These people possessed intellectual and creative capabilities and mental needs that were overlooked. The very concept of 'care' for the elderly should be redefined, as it implied so much more than physical needs. Above all we found the need and the possibility of 'learning'. Learning is a lifelong process. Old age is far more than loss and decay. And we should avoid the 'us' / 'them' thinking. The old person we see today is you and I tomorrow.

THE CENTRAL PART OF THE STORY

Narrative form and poetic language were the pillars of the project. As language is considered to be central in the learning process and interdependent with human thought (Vygotsky, 1992), creative writing and storytelling could be important

Ivor F. Goodson, Avril M. Loveless and David Stephens (Eds.), Explorations in Narrative Research, 21–32.

parts in an educational program for elderly people. Poetic language has an aspect of emancipation, and education at its best is also emancipating.

Aims and Objectives

Our focus on lifelong learning was not understood as an instrumental enterprise, or as education with a professional purpose, but more as an existential matter, as an enrichment of life. Writing, and storytelling, was a kind of exploration of life. Education of the elderly does not call for a new kind of 'special' education. Our aim was more than anything to view the education of this group in a *democratic* perspective—it was a question of inclusiveness. The oldest of us should be invited in, and be given an opportunity to, learn. We didn't view education in terms of 'upbringing' but more a need for re-education of generations who failed to see the resources in the oldest.

The concrete objectives of the project were:

1. We wanted to invite different groups of elderly people to join relatively long lasting courses in creative writing and storytelling;
2. We wanted to explore how this was experienced by the participants, and what characterised their texts.

No.1 was the practical and empirical part of the project; No. 2 was the research part.

Theoretical Inspiration

My own 'educational imagination' is particularly inspired by my encounters and conversations with three distinguished international educationalists. I have been influenced by the radical thinking of Elliot W. Eisner. In our field, Eisner's aesthetic perspective more than anybody stressed the important place of art in the hierarchy of knowledge. Art is, because it is focused on feeling, traditionally considered a seductive distraction, a contaminant in the development of intellect. But logic is only one of the ways in which rationality is expressed, and human intellectual capacity is far wider. We need alternatives to the prevailing domination of linear rationality in education. Rationality needs to be enriched by creative dimensions. Eisner stressed that affect and cognition were not independent processes, nor were they processes that could be separated. This is evident in a narrative. 'In narratives, whatever their subject, the rhythms of human feelings are never entirely submerged.' (Mc Evan and Egan 1995, p. VII). Eisner's original genre for evaluating educational quality—'educational criticism'—I would describe as a 'poetic narrative'. Eisner's aim of this special criticism was to expand our awareness of what we might not have noticed, and he defended narratives saying that stories got at forms of understanding that could not be reduced to measurement or scientific explanation (Eisner 1998).

Narratives, both fictional and 'real' are related to the forms of art, and they must not be reduced to decoration and entertainment; they can bring insight and development. 'Content and form shape one another', says Nussbaum (1990, p. 30).

Eisner (1992, p. 41) echoed this thought: 'In the arts and in much of life, the form something takes is very much a part of its content. In fact, what the content is often depends on the form it takes'.

This view, that form is an integral, inextricable part of the content, implies that form can and should be taught in educational work with narrative texts. In this, our approach differed from the tradition known as 'life histories'.

My inspiration also came from the phenomenologist Max van Manen. Merleau-Ponty said that 'Phenomenology, not unlike poetry, is a poetizing project' (quoted in van Manen, 1994 p. 13). A phenomenologist aims to return to the phenomena themselves by means of 'phenomenological reduction', and in letting the things speak 'just as we experience and encounter them: see, feel, hear, touch and sense them' (van Manen, 2001 p. 4). This is very similar to what a poet does. In poetry, the world is encountered afresh and created anew. The familiar is made strange and unknown, and vice versa. A phenomenological text is vocative: it speaks to us, we are then responsive; it also evokes a sense of *wonder*. Phenomenology finds its starting point in wonder, and it ends in wonder, more than in a clear conclusion.

A special form of narrative is the phenomenologist's use of *anecdote*, used as a rhetorical and methodological device (van Manen, 1994). 'The paradoxical thing about anecdotal narrative is that it tells something *particular* while really addressing the *general* and the *universal* (van Manen, 1994, p. 120; emphasis added).

The inspiration of Ivor Goodson[1] has been of particular importance. He reminds us of the story's oral roots, and in his own family and childhood culture he saw this universal human gift which could make the most humble illiterate person a true oral artist, an unforgettable storytelling star of the village. And even more important was Goodson's early discovery that storytelling was a form of *knowledge* that was linked to a matter of community consciousness. Through their storytelling people who were subjugated by social injustice had a feeling of independence. They were able to think for themselves and make their own critiques.

More than anything storytelling is involved in the building of an identity. Identity is an ongoing process. Identity is narrated, and it is open ended.

Our personal life as well as our professional life amongst other teachers' lives can be enlightened by narrative studies. Storying and narratology allow us to move beyond the main paradigms of inquiry—through their numbers, their variables, their psychometrics, their psychologisms and their de-contextualised theories. By using life histories we can understand how people live and learn in the life course. Such stories are lives interpreted and made textual—and we should explore the interconnections between life, narrative and learning. What do people learn *from* and *for* their lives by the autobiographical stories they tell? To find out more about this, we need to start developing a *theory of narrative learning*.

Goodson, a spokesman for the place of subjectivity in research warns us against celebrating the storying genre too uncritically, as it is far from politically neutral— it often supports the individualistic tendencies of our time. Free floating stories are not sufficient. A story cannot replace cultural and political analysis, but in a broader context it can be a good starting point for understanding how subjectivity is socially constructed. The great virtue of stories is that they particularise and make our experiences concrete. But the story is embedded in the history and the time. As researchers we have to locate as well as narrate.

Narratives are always linked to the question of power. We 'story' our lives, but we should always investigate where our 'storyline' comes from, and ask: Who gave me this 'script'?

These three perspectives are different, but they all question the absolute authority of 'objective' methodologies, and see the inadequacies of conventional, cognitive models. And they are all related to language, to a rhetorical dimension. Knowledge is not merely transmitted. The textual composition plays a crucial part, in life, research and art.

Education Methods and Principles

There were four teachers in the PEP group: Odd Saetre, Oddgeir Synnes, Mona Saele and I. At least two teachers were always present in the class. This helped the teachers to be observant, caring, and sensitive to the mood of the group and the individual students. Two of us, Synnes and I, carried out research based on the ongoing work in the groups. The biggest group had 12 participants and the smallest (the dementia group) had only three.

Special attention was paid to the creation of an atmosphere of safety, respectful communication, relationship building, humour, encouragement. The environmental setting was crucial.

The participants were usually given a topic to write about as 'homework' for each session. At the next session these tentative products were read aloud to the group, commented on, revised and improved. In the process we were careful about teaching them about rhetoric devices and the characteristics of different genres. Our purpose was learning.

We had a special focus upon the narrative/story, including the presentation of an oral story to an audience. It was never demanded that what they wrote or had to tell should be true or 'real', but inevitably in *all* texts their own life was transparent. The texts, from the very short *haiku* poems to long accounts were genre variations of life stories.

In our approach *evocation* was crucial—awareness and awakening. As topics for writing we used motivational starters, openings, headlines and sense stimulators.

The very first exercise started with their earliest memories. 'Close your eyes. Where are you, do you hear anything, voices… which colours do you see?' etc… Other starters could be a classic piece of music, a painting, a personal photo. To support the storytelling they could use an object: a piece of wallpaper, a medallion, a child's shoe… Or we started with a season or a colour—blue for example. Or we gave *one* word: 'silence', 'hands', 'return'. Or it could be *two* words: 'that day', 'the letter', 'the road', 'the door'—all very powerful starters. Sometimes the point of departure was a genre: a *haiku* poem, short story, fictive letter to a famous author, to an historical person, to the Prime Minister,[2] to an unborn great grandchild, to the future. Nature was a frequent theme; we dwelt with day and night: twilight time, sounds in the night, dawn, late summer days. We played with seeing things from a new perspective: as a snail sees it, the earth seen from space. Bertha let her old rose painted chest tell the family story on its journey through many generations, simultaneously weaving in the story of a nation's journey from poverty into oil and richness. The personal and the political went together.

A basic principle of ours was that of giving storytellers an audience. Stories must be shared. We live alone, we die alone, and we write alone. But a journey that is not *shared* is a poorer one. Reading and listening to the texts of other people enlarges our world, and sometimes these activities show us alternative worlds. To be 'seen' and 'heard' by others defines identity. This process does not end at a certain age. Something is added to my life if someone, with an open mind, listens to my story, hears my music, and sees what I have created. In a way this is simple and rather self-evident. But is this insight taken seriously in the care for the elderly in the modern western world? This is an area in which our project aimed at making a contribution.

Along with the principle of sharing, our principle of feedback/response was basic. Response had to come from the group—and the teacher(s). We insisted that the feedback should always have a positive focus. It was, however, wrong and showed a lack of respect not to have suggestions about improving the text. We never underestimated our learners. The aim was development and growth.

The dementia group needed a specific approach and a special awareness (Ådlandsvik, 2008). The work in this group was carried out in close collaboration with health personnel. One participant was always accompanied by a nurse, and sometimes spouses attended. The participants were too tired to write, but not for collective creating. We did the writing for them, and they had words, memories, and a life. Their former professional lives were in some cases starters. The pianist demonstrated and talked about his art; the housewife was able to describe what she used to do at home, and the very silent and depressed photographer taught with enthusiasm about how to compose a good picture. There must be balance between light and shadow, he told us, 'Without contrasts the picture becomes too flat'. We never forgot that. Together this 'creativity group' created texts about friendship, the rough ocean, the pale moon at daytime, the wise owl hooting in the night. The themes emerged spontaneously on the basis of conversation, music, moods.

Research Method (Reflection upon the Courses)

We found it natural to have a hermeneutic-phenomenological approach. We kept diaries, took notes before, during and after each session, and had conversations with the participants about the process and the products. We practiced participating observation.

Combining the role of the teacher and the researcher is a complex and risky enterprise. There is always a chance of being too positive about the findings. Poor results could be explained by poor teaching.

Statements and remarks were noted. Emphasis was put on awareness of, and in, 'the creative moment' and on sensitivity to words and their connotations. Phenomenological research is, not unlike poetry itself—a poetizing activity. In both cases the starting point was 'wonder'. 'Wonder is at the heart of the phenomenological attitude' according to van Manen (2005, p. 249). The researcher needs a special kind of openness, that of the poet—a sense of interpretative inquiry.

The texts from the groups provided us with a rich material to work with. We wanted to focus on the dimension of *meaning* for the participants, in our case, the meaning of verbal creativity.

Outcomes[3]

Many good texts were found. They are often direct in their expression, straightforward in style, with short sentences. The texts had 'empathic resonance', which means that they could inspire empathy and sympathy in ordinary people, but all texts are not necessarily so original. In very many cases the texts showed the positive aspects of life: harmony, peace, gratitude, reconciliation, wisdom, visions of the time to come. The tone of harmony impressed the younger readers, but we also noticed the bitter burden of war memories in these generations.

The consequences of the courses seemed to be *more than words*. One long lasting consequence was that of friendship. The groups offered opportunities for sharing memories, thoughts, experiences and company. There seemed to be a positive impact upon self esteem and belief in their own abilities and dispositions. Participants spoke of a new openness to: nature, details, colours, memories and language. 'I see the very small flowers along the way in a new way now,' was one statement. Even people with the beginnings of dementia showed a new, temporarily awakening.

In some cases there were signs of a 'healing' effect, even though we never intended to be therapeutic in our efforts. 'I cannot die yet, I have so many stories to tell, and at last somebody listens', were the words of Solveig, aged 91. Her nurse claimed that Solveig would have died weeks earlier than she actually did had it not been for the stories she wanted to tell. Of particular beauty was the love story of her life, about the handsome young man wearing his Stetson hat that lovely first spring evening, singing, 'Bergen, my home town'. Mette the humorist, 72, exclaimed: 'I have postponed my funeral; I can't miss the writing class!' Mette had discovered the power of poetic writing. In language she could now fly on a honeysuckle leaf under a pale blue summer sky and look down at the earth far below. And brilliant and bright Knut, 69, having Alzheimer's, had this comment as he pointed to his forehead: 'I need something for this one; I am tired of being met with pea-soup and sing song-activities at the old age centre. Here I am met with respect.'

A cancer patient had leave from the hospital to go to the course. He was truly a 'late bloomer'. 'The severe illness became easier to bear,' he expressed in a poem. His texts showed an intense joy and deep understanding. Never before was the grass so green and the autumn sky so clear. The 80-year-old man, a newborn excellent poet, wrote love poems with subtle erotic connotations. His doctors encouraged his participation in the writing group. And his 'class mates' could experience that death was natural, and that life has meaning even in the last days, which in fact became days of literary blossom—and blessing. Even old people have a future, even though it may be short. It is never too late for anything. In several cases we have experienced that texts from the course were referred to or read at the old person's funeral. This is a meaningful and dignified bridge between life and death and between those who left, and those staying behind.

Discussion and Ethical Implications

We had a very strong belief in the potential of the participants when we started, and we were not disappointed. In many cases our expectations were more than fulfilled. Positive expectations were an important element in our 'pedagogical creed', and in my view students are able to sense if this quality is present or not. Later, learning theorists like Albert Bandura stressed how crucial was a person's belief in his or her abilities. This belief is so important that it influences the results of the tasks performed. One of our learners, a very shy, old lady, described her own verbal development with sudden enthusiastic humour: 'I like this painter Salvador Dali. He says: If you think you are a genius, you become a genius!'

The role of an encouraging teacher in such a process, which is more important than the product, is evident. 'You flatter us too much,' was the comment from one of our learners. 'We don't quite believe what you are saying, but it does us *so* good; we are not used to it from school days or later studies. We are used to negative critiques, and that blocked our creativity.'

Meaningful learning processes also have an element of risk. It may be risky to let old people work with such themes as *'That day'*. For some people it brought back the memories of World War II. In several other cases it brought back that terrible day when a husband died suddenly. Tears were in the eyes in the group when such a story was read. But if our understanding was right, they were good tears, and they were shared tears.

We once met a question from a daughter about the danger of ending the course. What about that sudden empty feeling an old person could experience then? We had no sure answer—perhaps the families could help us in that.

Working with people with the beginning of dementia was especially ethically challenging. 'Dementia is the ultimate existential condition' (Killick, 2008, p. 5), involving the most fundamental philosophical question: *Who am I?* These people are struggling with their fragile identities and have a confused battle between the people they were and the people they are becoming—between dreams and daylight.

We have to consider whether we were in some sense exploiting old people for egoistic academic purposes in which publishing was a central part. The relation between the giver and the 'taker' of the story had to be examined. In our context we were teachers and also 'givers' to our aging students—in a sense we were door openers.

The process of aging shows a vast variety in health and interests. The older people are, the more different they become. There is loss, decay, loneliness and pain in old age, but also humour, hope and joy. Some of our learners would still have, maybe, 20 years to live. I fear there is some sad connection between loneliness in old age and untold stories. The working with, and sharing of, texts brings people closer to one another. People have opened doors to what is inside, they have left some footprints on this planet, and they are not so easily forgotten. We remember a text, a line, and we remember the person behind it.

The aspect of the freedom to learn, and freedom to choose what to learn, must be stressed. Creative writing is not the first choice for everybody, but neither is carpentry or computer study. But these age groups should be invited in, and be given an opportunity. Some of our participants hesitated at the start. What on earth was this? I am not a writer! 'We had to drag them in,' the nurse said. 'The last day of the group they had to be dragged out!'

More PEP Outcomes

Many more courses were held in the following years in Bergen and Hordaland County, led by some of the original teachers or by new ones. The people in one of the first classes still meet, more than a decade after the start. One group has lasted for six years, with the same teacher; another group kept on for years without any teacher—they taught each other, etc... Our efforts have inspired similar enterprises in Oslo and in other parts of Norway. Many courses for teachers who want to start new writing groups have been arranged. We had a sister project of PEP, named ERSK (Elderly People as a Resource in School Knowledge). In this context young and old people met to exchange stories, sometimes in a 'literary café'. Reciprocity in storytelling, both telling and receiving, was stressed in our approach. One important aim of the ERSK project was the development of mutual respect and understanding between the generations. Oddgeir Synnes[4] is carrying out his Ph.D. project on narratives by terminally sick and dying persons in a hospice context. Articles and books have been published; there have been academic conferences, symposia and there have been newspaper, radio and TV interviews, often including the students. Hordaland County established a website[5] with texts written by elderly people. The dementia part of PEP resulted in my contact with John Killick, Sterling University. He has for many years conducted a parallel work, but on a much larger scale. Killick (1997/2000) showed that the voices of people with dementia were poetic and could touch us deeply.

Despite being a successful project, with overwhelmingly satisfied participants and received with interest in the academic context, it still has a long way to go. This is not mainstream educational policy and theory—this is not strategic research. There are still attitudes to develop, and battles to be fought for priorities and funding.

The project has raised my awareness of the importance of understanding how important narrative is in the workings of the human brain. The PEP story convinced me that there is a lot of artistry in ordinary people's life and in the way amateurs are able to express it. Age does not necessarily set any limit. I have learnt that in the prevailing narrative of old people's place in our modern western society something is missing—a broader understanding of their (our) mental and creative needs and potentials, capacity for learning and the never-ending search for meaning in this mystery called life.

So What about the Story?

Creative storytelling in a classroom or in a nursery home and narrative research are of course different areas, but they have something in common—the purpose in both cases is learning and human development. This 'turn to narrative' could be said to be in fact a *return* to narrative (Ådlandsvik, 2005). Narrative seems to be a backbone human capacity. Poetry and narrative have been man's travel companions on the journey of life, through all ages and in all cultures. Narrative and teaching have been connected throughout the history of education. Moral values have been transmitted to the next generation by means of good examples. They have a stronger effect than abstract rules. A story appeals to our emotions. Real meaning—true insight is rarely dry.

One could object that an invented, fictional, 'creative' story is fundamentally different from a 'real' story, but that is not the case, and we could characterise the texts we received as 'faction'. *All* stories are created and the result of some kind of composition and the basis is life itself. What else could it be? In all cases the narrator *edits* and *selects* and these two aspects are decisive in the quality of the story and perhaps in some cases the quality of a person's life. And in our lives there are some elements we refuse to make part of our story.

So facts and fiction are not totally different worlds. A fictive story is an escape from reality—at the same time it explores and interprets reality. 'There is no clear disjunction between art on the one hand and life on the other' (McEvan and Egan, p. VIII). The aim is insight more than truth. A good story can say something true about life without being true, and truth can take the form of fiction. The most celebrated Norwegian novelists at the moment, Karl Ove Knausgaard, Per Petterson and Tomas Espedal are all 'writing their lives'.

All narratives carry moral messages in one way or the other and images of the moral world' says Ivor Goodson. (Goodson & Gill, 2011, p. 65).

A literary story has its own moral, which may differ from our everyday values. However, the best stories in the world of literature often deal with the battle between good and evil, and they sometimes carry an implicit imperative that things should be changed. But a good story is never moralistic. There is something left for the receiver to decide. You are led to the door, but it is up to you if you enter. You could call this 'The pedagogical space'. This is what makes the story a potent *learning device*, also for the reader.

The 'story must construct two landscapes simultaneously', according to Bruner (1986, p. 14)—the outer landscape of action and the inner one of thought and intention. Based on my own experience as a teacher and researcher I would say this continuously ongoing interpretative activity seems to be very central in the *learning process*, and it should be taken more seriously in the contemporary educational debate.

In the existential narrative process, in the interpretation of life, our inner and outer worlds penetrate each other. By narrative experience it is shaped and given meaning. There is an interactive relationship between the past and the present, and even the future is in a way involved. There is an ongoing dialogue between an earlier and later self.

The dialogue between the generations exemplified in our ERSK project illustrates Molly Andrews'[6]concept of 'intergenerational storytelling'. The stories from different age groups sometimes resonate with yourself, and when they are not at all on the same page that you know—they may be especially important to get.

Man's fundamental narrative capacity is hardly questioned today. But are we all storytellers to the same degree? There are researchers who argue that this capacity has more to do with a disposition—some are born listeners, and some are talkers.[7] In my view the pedagogic task is to develop both sides of the same person.

According to Goodson & Gill (2011) individual narrative 'character' differs from person to person. People have different 'narrative intensity' and different narrative strategies. Some are rather descriptive in their storytelling, others are more analytic and evaluative.

'Showing' is central in creative text composition, more important than 'telling' and explanation. But good 'showing' has an implicit interpretative and analytical dimension. The choice of words reveals what you have seen and understood.

A person's narrative capacity is naturally related to background and culture. However, it was not our experience that the best texts came from people with the highest formal education.

Our work with verbal creativity, focusing on detail, senses, and patterns seemed to make the world more visible to our aged students—but it also worked in another way. One of our participants said, 'The writing course brought me back to the person I used to be.'

So in many cases these aged amateur poetic writers became more visible to themselves. By the active sharing and commenting on texts they became more visible to one another and through different types of publishing the texts it could be that they even became more visible in the community. And work of this kind will hopefully contribute to make these age groups more visible in society as a whole.

THE STORY ENDS—AND CONTINUES

PEP has come to an end, but an end is sometimes a beginning. Last autumn we (the PEP teachers) were surprisingly invited to a book release in an island near Bergen. The author in question was one of our 'pioneer' students around a decade ago,

Esther, a farmer's wife, who all her life missed out on an education which her parents could not afford to give her. She is now 91.

The big room is crowded, and more chairs have to be carried in. The mayor is present to give a speech, and there are editors, journalists, musicians, neighbours, relatives.

Esther enters the stage, she needs some support. Our eyes meet. We share a story that has touched our lives, professionally or existentially.

With shy dignity Esther starts reading from and commenting on the thick book, the story of her life, based on texts of different genres, many of them from the PEP period. The title is *Writing, Days and Dreams*.

NOTES

[1] The following points of views related to Goodson are based on various books and papers and on dialogues we have had over the years in University of East Anglia and University of Bergen.

[2] In one case this letter was turned into an *authentic* one, with an Oslo address: 'Dear Jens...'

[3] A broader representation of 'results' or 'findings', including texts, is presented in Synnes et al., 2003.

[4] Synnes was the administrator and a particularly central and active member in the PEP group.

[5] Some texts are translated into English.

[6] 'The Symposium on Narratives, Context and Learning 16th and 17th May 2011', University of Brighton.

[7] Expressed in the symposium mentioned in note 6.

REFERENCES

Ådlandsvik, R. (Ed.) (2005). *Læring gjennom livsløpet (Learning through the life span)*. Oslo: Universitetsforlaget.

Ådlandsvik, R. (2007). Education, poetry and the process of growing old. *Educational Gerontology, 33,* 665–678.

Ådlandsvik, R. (2008). The second sight. Learning about and with dementia by means of poetry. *Dementia, 7*(3), 321–339.

Bruner, J. (1986). *Actual minds, possible worlds.* Cambridge, MA: Harvard University Press.

Eisner, E. W. (1992). The misunderstood role of the arts in human development. *Phi Delta Kappan, 73*(8), 591–95.

Eisner, E. W. (1998). *The kind of schools we need: Personal essays,* Portsmouth, NH: Heinemann.

Goodson, I. F., & Gill, S. R. (2011). *Narrative Pedagogy: life history and learning.* New York: Peter Lang Publishing, Inc.

Hustvedt, S. (2003). *What I loved.* London: Hodder and Stoughton.

Killick, J. (1997/2000) *You are words*: Dementia poems. London: Hawker Publications.

Killick, J. (2008). *Dementia diary. Poems & prose.* London: Hawker Publications.

McEwan, H., & Egan, K. (Eds.) (1995). *Narrative in teaching, learning and research.* New York: Teachers College Press.

Nussbaum, M. (1990). *Love's knowledge. Essays on philosophy and literature.* Oxford: Oxford University Press.

Synnes, O., Saetre, O., & Ådlandsvik, R. (2003). *Tonen og glaset. Pedagogisk arbeid med eldre og verbal kreativitet* (The tone and the glass: Educational work with elderly people and verbal creativity,. Kristiansand-S: Høyskoleforlaget.

Van Manen, M. (1994). *Researching lived experience. Human science for an action sensitive pedagogy.* London, Ontario: The Althouse Press.

Van Manen, M. (2001). Professional practice and 'doing phenomenology'. *Handbook of phenomenology and medicine,* 457–474. Dordrecht: Kluwer Press.

Van Manen, M. (Ed.) (2005). *Writing in the dark. Phenomenological studies in interpretive inquiry.* London, Ontario: The Althouse Press.

Vygotsky, L. (1992). *Thought and language.* London: The MIT Press.

AFFILIATIONS

Ragna Ådlandsvik

to us, then shaped through understanding, discussion and reflection (1998, pp. 22, 31).

We work up information, including the facts of our existence, into knowledge, much as a potter uses clay as her material which will be made into a piece of ceramics. Ideally, this process of transforming information into knowledge is what we as teachers help to foster in our classrooms.

Teaching which is built upon the importance of personal experience requires:

- An acute appreciation and acknowledgement of the importance of positioning: of the student, of the teacher, of the topic. All knowledge is situated—'there is no view from nowhere' (Nagel, 1986)—and the acquisition of knowledge is a fundamentally dynamic task. Recognising that knowledge bases are created and built up from particular positions, the classroom must be a space which uses rather than resists this locality. Moreover, questions of teaching 'marginalised youth' invitablity invite questions of boundaries: marginal to what/to whom? How are the categories of insider and outsider created and sustained in education? What can we do within our classrooms to make those boundaries more fluid, to shift the eyes of the beholder?

- Demonstrating that what is to be studied actually matters. It is not sufficient to assume that students will engage with the subject matter simply because not to do so will result in poor performance, and ultimately negatively impact upon life opportunities. Rather, curiosity needs to be ignited, and this is true for both teachers and students. A teacher who has grown numb to her subject matter is not one who will ignite a flame of intellectual passion in others. Interest and enthusiasm are not always contagious, but they are often so.

- Making connections between stories of the self and other stories, and ultimately to other forms of knowledge. While students' personal experiences are an important starting point for intellectual engagement, it is essential that they come to appreciate that individual stories are never just individual. While we are all of us unique, we can at the same time extract from concrete particulars to wider questions of culture and social structure. As Rice (2002) contends: 'The story of an individual life—and the coherence of individual identity— depends, for its very intelligibility, on the stories of collective identity that constitute a culture... cultures and societies organize individual identity' Individual stories reveal far more than their particular content. They also serve as an indicator of that which the speaker regards as 'tellable', and are created as a response to perceptions of audience. Moreover, and critically, individual stories can serve as the engine to social change. Not only telling one's stories, but hearing those of others, can be a critical moment in the awakening of a political consciousness, that is, realising that one's experiences are shared by others (and, by implication, might be at least partially a result of factors which extend beyond the self). In this way, the cultivation of narrative knowledge can be a primary means for exploring the relationship between structure and agency.

An especially fine-tuned ear listens beyond one's own horizon of experience. Individuals tend to tell stories only when they feel they will be listened to. Deep listening is, as Erika Apfelbaum (2001) argues, a 'risky business' for it requires individuals to entertain the possibility that the world is or can be a very different place to how one imagines it to be. This is why a good teacher is someone who is endowed with a rich imagination, not only with regards to his/her subject matter, but also in his/her ability to enter the world of those he/she wishes to teach. She must be willing to accept the possibility of profound differences between her real lived experiences and those of her students, and to think creatively how to bridge the chasm between those perspectives. Moreover, as Freire observes 'by listening to and so learning to talk with learners, democratic teachers teach the learners to listen to them as well' (1998, p. 65). The activities of listening and learning are integrally bound to one another and are demanded both of teachers and students in the transmission of knowledge.

STORIES AND TEACHING

In virtually every class I teach, I try not only to create an atmosphere in which students feel they can talk about their experiences in relation to the topics we are discussing, but also to build into at least some of the assessments a role for reflections of a personal nature. I will give two examples of this here. The first comes from my class on political psychology, where the first assignment for the class is to write an essay on their own political psychology. The instructions read:

> What are your political beliefs and where do they come from? Have these evolved over the course of your lifetime? What were the most significant influences on your political beliefs? How do these beliefs correspond to the actions in your daily life? What experiences have been most influential in forming your ideas, and why did you make sense of these experiences in the way(s) in which you did? What might have been another way of interpreting those critical experiences? What role did other individuals and/or groups play in the development of your political psychology? Using your own biography as a case study, examine how your experiences compare with a) the assigned readings b) outside readings c) class discussions and d) lectures. You will be assessed on your ability to apply key concepts and debates to your own life.

The second example comes from a class I teach on aging. Here, half of the course mark is based upon what I call an 'intellectual journal'. For each week's topic, I pose a number of questions which I ask students to respond to. The questions are rooted in the student's life experiences, but they must relate these questions to other course materials, including: readings, films, lectures and class discussions. Sometimes the journal questions require students to do a short practical exercise. Here is an example of instructions for the entry of the second week of the course, when the topic for discussion is 'the meaning of the category of age':

> Interview three people who are, from your point of view, 'young' 'middle-aged' and 'old'. Find out what 'age' means to the person with whom you are

speaking. What is their chronological age and what, if anything, does this age mean to them? These conversations do not need to be recorded, but you should take notes during and afterwards. Following this, write in your journal about the meaning of age and aging. How do your ideas compare with the people you interviewed? What is old? Are you old? What is the meaning of life in old age? In middle age? In youth? Moody (1991) suggests that we think about 'life as a whole' and focus on 'unity of human life'. What aspects of your life help you to do this? What hinders you? Is this a desirable goal, and is it realizable?

In both of these examples, my intention is to establish that students are, in themselves, people who come to us with experiences and certain kinds of knowledge, and that those are a valid foundation on which to build other kinds of knowledge. A vital part of my job, as I see it, is to provide them with tools which will help them to understand not only their own lives as they are living them, but also to imagine other ways of being, and ultimately to see and understand new aspects of the world in which we live.

In preparation for writing this chapter, I spoke with Agazi Afewerki[2] whom I originally met in Toronto 2009, at the conference on 'Marginalised Youth and Contemporary Education Contexts'. Agazi was one of the young people who was invited to tell the audience his story, how he had come up through the Pathways to Education programme[3] (http://www.pathwayscanada.ca/home.html), and had gone on to study first business, and then law. At the time he lived in London, England, where I teach). In our conversation, Agazi stressed time and again that the most important influence on his (highly successful) educational career was those teachers who had showed a real willingness to listen. Regardless of the subject matter, if a teacher were able to create in the classroom space for students' experiences to be validated—even if those experiences might not seem relevant—they fostered in the classroom an open, yet intellectually stimulating environment where real learning was possible. Much of what Agazi said echoed with my own experiences both as a student and now as a teacher. That it is not always possible to create such an environment is obvious; but too often it is the educational system itself which gets in our way. With the emphasis on pre-established, transparent learning objectives, we become less and less flexible as we enter the classroom, less open to how we approach the topics we wish to teach, and less sensitive to how certain discussions may engage or silence our students.

Narrative is an important tool for us to use in our teaching, in that 1) listening to the stories our students tell about their lives provides us with an insight into their worlds beyond our classroom. 2) equally, sensitizing ourselves to what stories are not not told in our classrooms is important. We must be forever vigilant about trying to make the space of our teaching an inclusive one. 3) people who tell stories about their experiences often, though not always, experience a sense of heightened agency. This comes not only from the experience of feeling listened to, but also from the shift of the location of the story from the realm of the individual to that of the collective. Ragna Ådlandsvik has argued that doors to learning can be opened if teachers can find the right keys. It is my belief that narrative is not the only key for the job, but it is a potentially significant one. We do aim to maximise the ability of our students to respond reflexively to the world(s) that we, in our teaching, endeavour to show them. This is not, however, the end of our teaching, but rather the diving off point.

LIMITATIONS OF PERSONAL STORYTELLING

What I have argued above notwithstanding, identifying our responsibilities as teachers, not in terms of those who have employed us but rather in terms of how we may best serve our students, can sometimes be akin to balancing on a tightrope. Not enough listening to your students, and appreciating the multiple layers of the worlds which they negotiate, can leave them, psychologically, outside of the classroom. The realities of their daily lives, their lived experiences, must be taken into account as we contemplate how best to teach them. Equally, their fears, and their dreams of worlds which they might inhabit, are important influences on what may or may not ignite or extinguish their curiosity. This has been the point I have been making up until now in this chapter. But counter-balancing this is my sense that we do our students a disservice if all we teach them is how to become increasingly self-reflexive. While I do have certain ideas about how a teacher might awaken an interest in her topic, I think it is also important to retain a sense of what it means to teach. I am there, in the classroom, with my students because I purportedly know about something. We have so far been focussing the discussion here on the 'how' of our students' knowing. But the 'what' of knowing should not be neglected. We find ourselves before them, in the classroom, because we have been deemed capable of teaching them. We have a duty to them, and to our profession, to get on with the job at hand.

When thinking about what teachers have been most inspiring for me in my educational career, it has not only been teachers who were interested in me and willing to listen to me, but also, and perhaps most importantly, those who were worth listening to, those who had a command of their subject, and who were determined that we would leave our lessons with them with some new knowledge. Inspiring teachers, in my experience, have always been very demanding teachers. They were not necessarily the teachers with whom one felt the most intimacy—some were more dispositionally inclined this way than others—but they were always teachers who pushed their students hard, and did their utmost to create an environment in which their high expectations could be realised. These teachers were not overly concerned with the personal tribulations of their individual students. But ironically, a classroom which is run with such a dedicated and conscious commitment to the task at hand—learning about a particular topic—has the potential to be very liberating for those who inhabit its space. Students who confront particularly challenging circumstances as part of their daily lives sometimes feel that they are released from the limitations imposed by their experiences. Inspiring teachers might be understanding, but they do not make excuses for their students, and they are realistic that the best way in which they can enable their students to progress intellectually is to help keep them focussed on their work. I have spoken about this apparent paradox with other colleagues, and I realise that I am not alone in my experience of tackling this conundrum: too little listening, you lose the student; but with too much emphasis on personal conversation, the student is denied access to the expertise of the teacher.

The German theologian and philosopher Freidrich Schleiermacher, writing in the 18th century, commented on the extreme importance—and rarity—of the skill of lecturing, going so far as to say 'the true and peculiar benefit a university teacher confers is always in exact relation to the person's proficiency in this art' (cited in Murphy, 2010, p. 129). Indeed, he went so far as to argue, 'It is worth the trouble to reserve this form of instruction always for those few who, from time to time, know how to handle it correctly' (p. 129). While his position, as stated here, assumes a strong form of articulation, anyone who has endured the plague of our modern times—death by PowerPoint—will recognise in it some truth[4]. The problem which Schleiermacher identified more than 200 years ago is very much alive today, but is rarely a topic of discussion amongst academics. While all those who teach at university are expected to deliver lectures—and indeed are even called lecturers—how this mode of delivery might or might not engage students is a relatively neglected subject. Schleiermacher made a critical distinction between transmission and production of knowledge, arguing that lecturers should seek not to impart knowledge per se, but rather to 'reproduce their own realisations so that the listener may constantly not simply collect knowledge but rather directly observe the activity of 'reason' as it creates knowledge'. (Murphy 2010, p. 108) Thus the primary function of a professor is 'not to transmit knowledge but to provide an observable and imitable model of how to produce knowledge' (p. 108). We as teachers must invite our students into the worlds of our own scholarly endeavours giving them insight into the intellectual journey we have followed, so that ultimately they might see with us what we see in our scholarly pursuits.

This does not sound so very far off from my own model of teaching and learning, discussed in the earlier passages in this chapter. We as teachers must stay connected to and engaged by our disciplines, and far from there being a virtually impassable gulf between our teaching and our research, these aspects of our professional lives must be linked as much as is possible. But how, the reader might question, do we reconcile this with the current demands put upon us? The increasing movement towards standardisation in the classroom means that educators are forced to produce a 'one size fits all' lecture.

In a recent interview with the philosopher Mary Warnock, she spoke to me about some of her concerns with the current state of education in Britain. She said:

> I think the trouble is that there's not time for most teachers to explore or really get to know what will fire off their individual pupils, and I think this is one of the troubles, so that it becomes just a form where you hand out, like handing out a bit of paper, to a whole class...the same bit of paper to a whole lot of people.

Teaching takes time, and in our age of dwindling resources, where we are always being asked to do more with less, time is an increasingly scarce commodity. But it is time—the ability to be in time, take time, continuity over time—that lies at the heart of our ability to be effective teachers and careful listeners. It remains to be seen what will become of our profession as the rich ground required for intellectual exchange becomes ever more starved of nourishment.

CONCLUDING THOUGHTS

At a conference on educating marginalised youth in Canada in which I participated (and upon which the special issue of *Education Canada*—where parts of this chapter first appeared, was built), the presenters spent a day in conversation with one another. We were all asked to write a few words in response to the question 'What do you believe to be true but can't substantiate?' I would like to conclude this chapter with my response to this question, as scribbled on my workshop papers:

I believe that everyone is born with the potential to be curious about the world around them and beyond. It is our job as educators to ignite that curiosity and to provide students with the skills to explore it. This creative act of making meaning (which includes but is not limited to investigating our own position in the world, and enhances the possibility of realising our own potential) is one of the core activities that identify us as being human.

NOTES

[1] This chapter appeared previously in the journal *Education Canada* (2010), vol 50, number 5, pp. 27–30, as part of a special issue on 'Marginalised Youth: A Tranquil Invitation to a Rebellious Celebration.' It is reprinted here with permission from the Canadian Education Association.

[2] Agazi Afewerki and Mohammed Shafique founded YEP (Youth Empowering Parents), aimed at providing basic tools for cultural integration. The programme was recently selected for a Intercultural Award from the United Nations. Out of more than 400 applications from 60 countries, ten were successful. For more about this programme, please read 'The unique status of marginalization: The birth of Youth Empowering Parents (YEP)' in Tilliczek, Kate and Ferguson, Bruce, eds. (forthcoming) *Youth, Education and Marginality: Local and Global Expressions.* Wilfrid Laurier University Press, Waterloo, Ontario, Canada.

[3] 'Pathways to Education' is a programme which was established by the Canadian government in 2001 to tackle the high secondary school drop-out rate in eleven of its most economically deprived neighbourhoods. The programme has had great success, reducing the drop-out rate by as much as 70%, and dramatically increasing the levels of youth continuing on to post-secondary education. For more information on this programme, visit (http://www.pathway scanada.ca/home.html)

[4] Some Powerpoint slides are wonderfully creative, helping the audience to distil, and sometimes visualise, the meaning which may be buried in hundreds of words. However, this benefit is obscured when slides are merely read aloud, word for word, to a defenceless audience, who must resign themselves to be treated as if they are incapable of reading the words for themselves.

REFERENCES

Apfelbaum, E. (2001). The dread: An essay on communication across cultural boundaries, *International Journal of Critical Psychology, 4*, 19–35.

Freire, P. (1998). *Teachers as cultural workers: Letters to those who dare teach,* Translated by Donoldo Macedo, Dale Koike, and Alexandre Oliveira. Boulder. CO: Westview Press.

Moody, H. (1991). The meaning of life in old age. In N. Jecker (ed.) *Aging and ethics: Philosophical problems in gerontology.* New Jersey: Humana Press.

Murphy, P., Michael P., & Marginson. S. (2010). *Imagination: Three models of imagination in the age of the knowledge economy.* Oxford: Peter Lang.

Nagel, T. (1986). *The view from nowhere.* Oxford: Oxford University Press.

Rice, J. S. (2002). Getting our histories straight: Culture, narrative, and identity in the self-help movement. In J. Davis (ed.) *Stories of change: Narrative and social movements.* Albany, NY: SUNY Press.

AFFILIATIONS

Molly Andrews
Centre for Narrative Research,
University of East London

5. NEGOTIATION AND RENEGOTIATION
OF GENDER IDENTITIES

Narratives of Two Hong Kong Teachers

INTRODUCTION

A wealth of literature on gender identities undertaken by western research communities shows that gender scripts have real consequences for male and female teachers' identity constructions. Social expectations and stereotyped images of men and women teachers affect teachers' gender identities as well as their professional experiences and opportunities (Biklen, 1995; Casey, 1990; Coffey & Delamont, 2000; Smedley, 2007; Tamboukou, 2000; Wayne & Blye, 2006). There has been growing research efforts into research on Chinese women primary teachers (Chan, 2004; Luk-Fong, 2010). Little published work on Hong Kong Chinese men and women secondary teachers has been found. Understanding teachers' gender identity is important because the way gender dynamics has worked to shape teachers' gender identities in their school days may yield results for the students they interact with. Sabbe and Aelterman (2007), in their comprehensive review on gender in teaching, rightly spell out that 'teaching is historically and culturally imbued with multiple discourses and subjectivities of gender' (p. 529).

This chapter portrays gender identity construction, negotiation and renegotiation of two Hong Kong Chinese teachers, Shuijing and Baibin, who both have been involved in painstaking struggles with their gender identities but with varied learning backgrounds. Their narratives aim to illuminate understanding of:

- How the gender identities of the Hong Kong Chinese male and female teachers were negotiated and renegotiated, their varied institutional experiences, and;
- Crucial elements contributing to gender identity negotiations.

THE LIFE HISTORY APPROACH

The portrayals of the two cases were drawn from the data of a qualitative study of 12 female and 12 male teachers in secondary schools from 2007 to 2008. The life history study aimed at understanding how men and women teachers' gender identities were negotiated and constructed in changing social historical contexts in Hong Kong. Two interviews, each of which lasted from 90 to 150 minutes, were conducted with each informant individually to collect their full life history, with a focus on their gender identity development (Goodson and Sikes, 2001). A focus group interview in groups of three to five was conducted three to six months after

Ivor F. Goodson, Avril M. Loveless and David Stephens (Eds.), Explorations in Narrative Research, 43–58.

the individual interview. The purpose was to facilitate the informants' discussion of the broad themes arising from the individual interviews and reflect on the process of the experiences of participating in the research (Morgan, 1998).

In line with the tradition of narrative studies, the storied evidence collected through conversation interviews is not so much a focus on its chronological or 'historical truth' as on the current, subjective meaning of the life events of the informants (Josselson, 2006; Spence, 1982). On the other hand, narrative studies following a life history approach give equal respect to both subjectivity and inter-subjectivity (Goodson and Choi, 2008). Documentary analysis, such as artefacts, social policy document and relevant literature, is carried out by the life history researchers in order to unfold the cultural context in which the storytellers' life events are located (Polkinghorne, 2007). Thus the informants' interactions with the contexts and constructions in which their gendered identities are embedded can be illuminated.

Data shows that while there are traces of gender stereotyping in the sample of teachers, a striking majority of them demonstrated a variety of negotiations in cross-sex options, in the wider contexts of traditional Chinese and hybridised Hong Kong gender systems. The selection of Shuijing and Baibin for the portrayal of gender negotiation of male and female teachers in this chapter is based on certain theoretical and practical considerations. The choice of different sexes as cases allowed me to explore the similarities and differences of gender identity construction between male and female teachers. In view of the limited space and the need to provide evidence-based arguments confidently for readers to judge the plausibility of the interpretation, a small number of cases were deemed more feasible. Shuijing and Baibin were selected because their gender negotiation process demonstrated the 'efficacy' of life stories, which had a rich potential for enhancing our understanding of negotiations and learning (Goodson, Biesta, Tedder and Adair, 2010).

GENDER IDENTITIES

While socialization theorists emphasise the moulding force of social institutions, researchers in line with constructivism argue that agency accompanies gender construction, although social institutions and other factors restrict them from choosing freely.

Children are able to establish the basic gender identity that 'I am a boy' or 'I am a girl' at three but it is not until several years later that they understand their sex. This remains invariant and regardless of changes in surface appearance like hair length (Egan and Perry, 2001). However, gender identity undergoes modification and expansion in their daily interaction with the family, schools, the media, the broader community, workplace and other social institutions (Munro, 1998). It is shaped by social factors as well personal negotiations (Archer, 1999; Connell, 1996; Moschella, 2006).

Lewin (1984) suggests that concepts of masculinity and femininity involve people's beliefs in their own competencies as males and females. These beliefs, however, are derived from personal and idiosyncratic rather than the stereotypical gender attributes. Gender identity has a varied impact on one's personal identity. Hoffman (2006) suggests that people's gender self-confidence is affected by the extent people accept their gender attributes, and how importantly people attach their femaleness and maleness to their personal self. Studies on gender identity development shows that women's healthy gender identity development involves movement from an externally and societally based definition of womanhood to an internal definition grounded in 'the woman's own values, beliefs, and abilities' (Ossana et al., 1992, p. 403). Rebecca, et al. (1976) suggests that people can progress from a lack of awareness of gender role, through a polarization stage in which traditional sex roles are adopted, till the final stage where the stereotyped gender roles are transcended. By the final stage, people are able to perceive their own qualities as a 'human' rather than as a 'female' or 'male'.

Gender Identities Development in Hybridised Hong Kong Society

Sex characteristics do not vary substantially between different societies but the gender system can vary in different cultures and societies. The traditional Chinese gender system is asymmetrical, dominated by male power (Chow, 2000; Luk-Fong, 2010). A son carries on the family surname and the honour of the clan and thus enjoys a much higher status than a daughter, who has to adopt the surname of her husband. The traditional 'three obediences' of Chinese women to 'follow their father, their husband and their son' at different phases of their life cycle is indicative of the women's partial membership to the social order (Ko, 1994). Proper masculinities in traditional Chinese society involve honouring one's ancestors and shouldering the responsibilities of preserving an extended family. Femininities refer to being submissive and supporting men to look after the household (Luk-Fong, 2010).

As a Special Administrative Region of China, 95 percent of Hong Kong's population are of Chinese ethnic origin but the city has long been considered a metropolitan city where cultures of the East and West meet. It has been commented that there was no indigenous Hong Kong culture before the nineteenth century (Leung, 1996). Hong Kong was mainly a city of refugees who fled from the Chinese mainland, thus bringing with them the traditional Chinese culture. However, when Hong Kong was ceded to Britain by the Qing dynasty government in 1842, the British rule made western culture ingrained in the traditional Chinese values, generating a 'distinctive indigenous' (Lau & Kuan, 1988) or 'hybridised' (Luk-Fong, 2010) Hong Kong culture. Conventional Chinese values and western cultures co-existed in various forms.

Studies published in the 1980s show that children in Hong Kong are socialised in the traditional ideal of gender roles through play; boys are given active toys such as guns and trains while girls are expected to play with dolls and kitchen utensils (Luk, 1981). The educational system was supposedly westernised under the British rule. Sons and daughters had equal opportunities in education, especially after the implementation of compulsory education in the 1970s. Yet schools were still found to be reinforcing gender stereotypes. Males were generally described in terms of competency and strength while females were characterised by warmth and expressiveness. Boys were often ashamed when assigned to the Arts class to do the 'girls' subjects (Luk, 1981). Gender role identity and stereotypes are found more distinct among primary and secondary students (Cheung, 1986).

Opportunities for women's participation in economic activities increased in the 1980s when Hong Kong rapidly transformed to a service economy. Against the backdrop of Deng Xiao-ping's 'Open Door Policy' in China at the end of 1978, Hong Kong's integration with the mainland accelerated and regained it its traditional role as the country's main provider of commercial and financial services (Schenk, 2008). At the same time, gender equality, discrimination, and inclusivity became core issues in education reforms. Female students often outnumbered male students admitted to the university through the 'Early Admissions Scheme' (i.e. secondary six school students with the HKCEE Ordinary Level Examination or good results at secondary six could be admitted to universities one year earlier, without taking the A Level Examination), contributing to a phenomenon that there were more female students at university, even in some traditional male dominant faculties, like Chemistry and Medicine (Feng, 2011). Nevertheless, despite objective changes concerning women in Hong Kong, including their socioeconomic participation, educational attainments and family structure, gender identities and stereotypes, they were still found lagging behind in many social aspects (Cheung, et al., 1997).

Portrayal of Gender Identity Negotiations

It is the purpose of this chapter to illuminate the development of the gender identities of Shuijing and Baibin who were brought up in the 1960s and 1970s in the hybridised cultural context of Hong Kong. Gender identity is always in the process of negotiation and renegotiation (Hall, 1990). The sections below portray some critical moments where negotiations were more evident in their life stories. Some of the tensions in power struggles and gender self definitions could only be recognised many years later upon their self-reflection. The moments of Shuijing and Baibin's negotiation of their social institutional experiences are presented in parallel.

Shuijing in her family   Shuijing is the youngest daughter in her family. She has an elder brother and sister. She had a strong wish to be a boy throughout her childhood as she considered boys had more privilege and freedom to choose 'rough games'.

> I hung around more often with my elder brother. My elder sister is very feminine. She likes Hello Kitty but I've never seen why it is attractive!... Few people told me I was pretty when I was a child and I didn't expect anybody to do so (individual interview).

Shuijing has both successful and unsuccessful negotiations of her gender identities in childhood with regards to play.

> My parents did not restrict my choice of toys or extra-curricular activities on the whole. But they forced me to wear dresses. My mum also did not allow me to learn Taekwondo (individual interview). I wanted to learn Taekwondo but my brother said it was dangerous. This made me become more eager to be a boy (focus group).

Shuijing does not cry easily.

> From when I was three years old my father was not with us in Hong Kong. He came home when I was in Primary One. Each time, he stayed with us for one to two weeks. So I was very distant from my father. Actually I was a bit scared of him... My mum was sort of neurotic. When I got angry with myself and locked myself in my room, she was very worried. I wished she could leave me alone. I didn't want to cry in front of her. I forced myself not to cry as this worried her. I don't think it is a gender matter. That is the way I expressed myself (individual interview).

In order not to worry her mother, Shuijing reacts strongly to 'feminine expressions' such as tears or screams.

> To a certain extent I'm tough. Say if a boy cries, I'll demand how come, he as a boy, cries. I'll let girls cry for a while (individual interview). I'm also scared of flying cockroaches. But I just CAN'T scream... Why am I highlighting this? Because many boys in my school just scream away when they see cockroaches. They scream when they see something terrible or funny. These images of boys are new to me (focus group).

Baibin in his family   Baibin is the eldest son in the family. He has a younger brother and sister. When Baibin talked about his family, a lot of it related to his mother but he concluded about his father in just one sentence.

> My mum is very masculine—because my dad didn't play his father's role properly—this is all I want to say. I could see how tough my mum is. My grandmother was a typical traditional Chinese woman who valued sons and devalued daughters. My mum had to sacrifice her education opportunities. She worked in a factory at a very young age and supported my two uncles' tuition fees. That's why she is very independent (individual interview).

Baibin was 'skinny' and suffered from asthma right up to early adolescence. His mother was the first one who said he looked like a girl because of his fair complexion. He was very conscious of not displaying typical male attributes and behaviour, including his voice, complexion and temperament.

> I don't know why. I just can't help but feeling sick when I see little crawling insects. My younger brother is absolutely fearless of them... When I was a small boy, I saw an insect creeping about in my bathing tub, and I screamed

and dashed into the sitting room, naked. I was so embarrassed and my parents were grinning and said that I was an idiot (individual interview).

Baibin strived to become a responsible young 'man' in his childhood and had some success.

I shouldered the responsibilities in my (original) family. I made efforts to take up the role of an eldest brother. I helped cook dinner for my family when I was just about ten. Later I made breakfast and lunch and sometimes even dinner on my own... all compelled by my family conditions... I tried my best to make my mum happy. I was very successful... Sometimes I did the art assignment for my younger brother as I was rather talented in drawing. His teacher complemented him on the printings and I felt I'd fulfilled the eldest brother's role... I think these are the masculine parts of me... to take up the burden and not to trouble others (individual interview).

Shuijing in education institutions Shuijing found her school years the most painful in her life.

To me being a 'tomboy' is acceptable, because that's me. But I hated my primary classmates calling me a 'manly witch', which is an insult to my outward appearance. I think I am active, a bit straightforward and I am tough in certain aspects (individual interview).

My mum got me into a girls secondary school, with the hope that I would be more feminine. I had short hair when I was in Secondary One. There were times when I went into the toilet and the girls all fled. Sometimes they mocked at me, saying that I had no need to comb my hair. Then sprinted away... I had very strong feelings of being isolated, deserted... My classmates didn't know whether to take me as a boy or a girl. In terms of identity, I felt very marginalised and my self-image was poor. I was very withdrawn and thought I was useless. I was very conscious of others' comments. During summer holidays I mainly spent my time alone at home, plain and safe, in a closed environment. There was no such thing as romance at all (individual interview).

I seldom said anything—sometimes for a few days. My classmates were nosy, chatterboxes, enjoying idle gossip all day long. I had no way of joining in (focus group).

Shuijing worked hard to fit in with her peers in the later secondary school years by acquiring some girlish gimmicks, although she felt she was not being herself.

I had an impression that it was at a later stage that I learnt to chat about pop singers with my classmates... We formed a group called 'Seven Sisters' but I did not feel really at ease with this (individual interview).

The turning point of Shuijing's negotiation of gender identities was when she did her teacher education.

At college my femininity stood out because there were guys. I had strong feelings of being a woman. I was sensitive to others' feelings. I noticed many female colleagues shared these attributes. At that time, those guys were rather suppressive but I did not want to suppress myself. When my female colleagues wanted to share their feelings with me, they found me very empathetic. I thought perhaps that was my femininity... Thank God I finally got to know some girls like me—they went hiking with me and joined the Environmental Protection Society. We shared some of our dreams—like when we learnt to drive. Those were topics I couldn't find anyone to share with in my secondary school (focus group).

One of my female friends in college is very feminine but she could sometimes be rather boyish. She accepted my style, like absentmindedness and silliness. She did not gossip. I gained more self confidence after three years of college life. Interaction with female colleagues with different personalities was helpful. As there were more females than male students in teacher education institution, I became more certain that it was my character rather than my gender that made me what I was...

I became a Christian in Year Two. I joined a cell group. I was still a 'tomboy'. Male group members were in the minority but they were open to sharing their feelings. They were able to express freely their struggles or unhappiness. Other members didn't find them strange. Therefore my fear of people gradually faded and I was more courageous in handling my problem. Perhaps I came late to adolescence and starting to think about the problem of my gender identity. I had a strong desire to change my state of being...

In fact I made great efforts to rescue my female gender identity. I remember I joined a gender workshop and one of the activities was to look at the mirror and tell myself 'I am a woman'. It was so difficult for me. But finally I tried to do it... If you asked whether I really wanted to be a woman? I would say I hope to find a balance. I wanted to sort out the bad feelings and my messy gender identities... after I was discovered and supported in the cell group, I was relieved.

One day I said to myself—why not keep my long hair? I think that marked the day I didn't mind being a woman anymore (individual interview).

Baibin in education institutions Baibin considers himself 'more like a girl than a boy' before he went to university.

I was rather tall—very skinny and fragile. My female classmates always asked if I was ill... This is not what I expected of a male (focus group).

Some guys in primary schools made fun of me. I did not take them seriously. But I became self conscious when my Chinese Language teacher made a similar remark. I think now that it was because the two women who I respected most in my life said I was like a girl that I had become more and more doubtful about my gender identity...

I was no good at football, or bad language. I just couldn't bring myself to do all that. Some guys mocked me and asked me to play with girls—I felt very bad in those days... I was one of the 'scholarly types'—sentimental, fond of Chinese literature, fiction, could cry—but afraid to be noticed by others (individual interview).

Baibin could not identify a sufficient amount of gender-congruent attributes to feel comfortable with his gender. He suffered from asthma right up till his early adolescence. He made great efforts to do physical exercise and gradually achieved a 'manly physique'. He also chose the boy scouts as an extra-curricular activity that could develop his masculinity.

I deliberately joined the Boy Scouts in my secondary year. On those outings, I was forced to face difficulties and there was no way of escaping... I hoped to become more independent and mannish. I became aware of similar motives many years later. I realised that a uniform was a strong symbol of power (individual interview).

I joined the Boy Scouts because I thought a man should be as strong as a soldier. I didn't find it very successful because every year I met some boys who were very masculine and I felt inferior to them (focus group).

Baibin's negotiation of a masculine gender identity was shaped by social comparisons within the traditional social and cultural norms.

I think my choices at secondary school were correct because I was good at literature. I tended to be sentimental. But I did have a struggle at that time— boys took sciences and the arts was for girls (focus group).

Just like Shuijing, Baibin was able to build up a certain amount of gender self-confidence at university.

I was elected as the Chairman of the Chinese Society. I tried my very best to play the role of a good man. The whole association was in my hands. Once I attended the joint association meetings in the Student Union. After the meeting, people said that the chairman of the Chinese Society was the best-looking and the most articulate. I was relieved! This did help build up my confidence in my later teaching years (individual interview).

However, he also experienced an important challenge which reinforced his sense of inadequate masculinity:

A professor in my department was found to be involved in a sexual harassment case. That was my first year at university but I had to take on the responsibility of handling it—because I was the chairman! All the students were shocked. I received a letter from the professor. I received a letter from the victim. Finally the dean intervened and I was asked to release an

'Apology' with a view to getting rid of him... It was very, very difficult for me (individual interview).

Shuijing in the workplace Shuijing has been teaching for 13 years in two secondary schools—the first a co-ed school and the second a boys' school. She thought she did 'quite well' there, namely because her students seldom found her to be very masculine. She also did not like being 'too feminine'—her female gender identity was fortified later at the boys' school.

I had to teach the boys not to use dirty words in front of girls. And when they shared with me their love affair troubles, I talked to them from the perspective of a woman...

I enjoy the privilege of being a woman. Male teachers have to do 'labour intensive' work and not as mean... battling with female colleagues. I do enjoy this side of things... Some male colleagues did say some nice things about me... I was not used to that at the very beginning—but I got used to it because they were genuine compliments. I also realised that I had a good pair of long legs (individual interview).

The negotiations went on in the workplace with regard to the style of interaction between other male and female teachers.

We had six staffrooms and in my room they were all female. I couldn't stand staying in that group of people for too long. Therefore I became a 'bad woman' because I was often searching through a different staffroom for colleagues to eat out with. Because I drove and drank red wine I was a 'bad woman'. I seem to have rocked the boat... There was some gossip. Some colleagues had the viewpoint that a woman should stay at home, and not answer back whatever the men crack...

I was unhappy for a while. Now we have all made some adjustments. They gradually got to know I had strong character but not a hot temper. I also began to understand why they reacted like that. Although I am a person who likes physical touch, I have learnt to be more sensitive to invisible boundaries. When I put myself in the shoes of those middle managers, I realise that these were all wives. They probably got very disturbed if suddenly a woman hung about with their husbands. This did not happen in my first school—the male colleagues went to pub with me. There are many subtle cultures in the workplace—so I have to adjust (focus group).

Baibin in the workplace Baibin taught briefly in a primary school before he moved to the current secondary school where the pay was better. He has had about 20 years of teaching experience. Teaching was not an occupation Baibin liked best. He even held a view that men with aspirations should not teach—or at most teach for one to two years and then go beyond the teaching environment.

> My best subject at university was fiction writing. But to be a writer in Hong Kong is to be poverty stricken sooner or later... I became a teacher because of the financial considerations of my family (individual interview).

Teaching is a female job and Chinese literature is a feminine subject in school. Baibin tried to change his calligraphy style because his was as elegant as a female's. This led to a certain new understanding of his own character.

> People asked if the scripts I wrote were written by a girl. Teachers have to write on the board. I was conscious of this to the extent that I tried to change my way of writing. But it didn't work. I found that one's style of script reflects the heart (individual interview).

Baibin was confident in his teaching abilities and received some very positive comments from his students. They found him good at explaining things clearly and said his teaching style was lively. Nevertheless, he was not satisfied with his role as a head of department.

> Although I am now in a middle leader position, I wish I could just follow behind somebody and be a supporter... I learnt that many female colleagues did not want to be the head. Their aspiration was to marry a good husband and have few work burdens... I tended to be too lenient and care for the feelings of my colleagues (individual interview)

> I don't look like a head of department. I hate asking people to do something they don't want to do. Other heads have an entirely different approach. Our Principal actually wants us to be more managerial, cold-blooded, even. But I just can't. Perhaps it's because I studied Chinese and have been since childhood very sensitive to human relations... I sort of have the 'kindness of an ignorant woman'...

> When do I feel like a man in the department? It's when the publishers send in desk copies. The ladies will ask me to carry those books and I don't mind doing that for them (focus group).

Shuijing in a male-female relationship Shuijing fell in love with a colleague in the second school but the relationship terminated two years later, after he left the school.

> I did find that I could be very feminine and play the woman. This was what my boyfriend said. We had a good physical relationship. It was beyond my boyfriend's expectations. Perhaps it's because I was used to having a lot of physical contact with my mum... When I was upset, I would tell him that I wanted to see him. I think it's the right of a girlfriend...

> We were in the same school. I'm very particular about tidiness and he was notoriously messy. I expected him to agree with me. Sometime we couldn't help but criticise each other. This was very hurtful. I'm not sure if I learnt anything from our relationship. But at least it helped to develop my female side (individual interview).

Baibin in a male-female relationship   Many women can share their inner feelings with me. They found me more approachable... unlike many domineering men...

> I was my wife's first lover... We got to know each other at university. She majored in English. What impressed me most was when I saw her reprimanding the members of an association meeting. I thought she suited me and at that time I liked strong women. I sometimes think I am very indecisive... But later I realised I had got it wrong. She liked taking a dependent role, but I was not aware of this when we started dating—only after we married I realised. I wanted to share my burdens with her but in actual fact she expected me to take on hers more often than not...

> I initiated the separation. I thought this would be good for both of us. I could not play the role of a good husband and I even lost my temper... I didn't understand her. Neither did I understand myself! Many male colleagues of my age are very successful in their male roles and enjoy their family lives. I am a bit lost and am always asking myself why I am failing as a man... In the end I found that marriage didn't suit me... I chose to run away—avoid the big challenges. Men should not be like that (individual interview).

Current Gender Self-definition

The 30 to 50 years of lived experiences recalled by Shuijing and Baibin respectively show that gender identities are constantly in the process of negotiation. I will first describe both their past and current gender self-definition, followed by a discussion of the crucial elements that contributed to these Hong Kong teachers' gender identities.

Shujing

> I have only begun to feel good about myself in the last three to five years. I have more or less now got a balance between my masculine and feminine characteristics...

> I realise there's something in me that won't change. For example I don't wear 'those clothes'. But that isn't a problem. My way of walking is not very feminine and I'm sort of a bit care free... I like to feel free. But I'm not mannish. You can see that from my choice of outfits...

> Now I realise that I would rather be rational and rationality is not something that only applies only to men. It is something gained from life experiences and learning, from my education. It belongs to me. I have come to see myself as having some masculine strengths, such as being tough—I do not give up easily—although I am still rather fragile and easily get hurt in many ways...

> A true woman is 'very feminine, willing to sacrifice and be accommodating but not with her own values, i.e. *wai rou nei gang* (with inner toughness residing in outer tenderness)'. I am still learning to be tender and considerate.

Shuijing has become more self-accepting of her appearance and personality although she defines herself as not yet being 'a real woman'. She has been able to appreciate some of the qualities which used to be considered incompatible with her sex—as part of what she is. She sees 'manly' toughness as her asset and rationality as not just the attribute of men. However, tenderness and the willingness to sacrifice were still defining feminine attributes that Shuijing identified for his continuing learning process.

Baibin

> I pay a lot of attention to my outfits and don't find this obsessive. I believe all human beings enjoy beauty. Perhaps I am influenced by some of the elementary philosophy I studied before. Masculine and feminine beauties make a perfect blend—this applies to many aesthetic objects or phenomena...

> I wish I could be what people regard as upfront and bold. I play the roles of a man poorly. I suppose I just get a pass grade for being a man—six marks out of ten—because I am not responsible enough as a leader in my department... Men should take a stronger leadership than women in secondary schools. I expect men to be able to cope with more stress and remain calm in tackling difficulties. Men should shoulder more responsibilities than women. These are what a man should do... I am not ambitious and don't like power games...

> I am not sure how woman-like I am... but I do hope to have somebody to depend upon in the future. Even now, I still doubt my gender identity.

Baibin sees himself as not fitting into his gender category and is ambiguous about his masculine image and capabilities. His subjective judgment of his body image and personality is not entirely positive. His definition of *dazhangfu* (a true man) is congruent with the traditional Chinese value—that men should be stronger than women. Men have to play a leadership role and shoulder more responsibilities, in the family or in the workplace. Although he managed to live up to such a standard and gained more gender self-confidence when he took up the leadership responsibilities of a chairman in a student association of the university, he still felt conscious of his inner preference for having someone to depend on in his marital relationship. Such a tendency is considered a feminine attribute—disgraceful for a man to have. Nevertheless, Baibin feels at ease with his interest in his attire and is able to appreciate his expressive abilities.

Crucial Elements Contributing to Gender Identity Negotiation

Politics of narration Shuijing and Baibin have experienced obvious struggles in resolving their conflicts about gender, including for example, how well they can fit the sex they were born into and how they can live at ease with attributes they have that are perceived as incompatible with their gender type. Negotiation is the process by which individuals take up certain positions in a power relationship (Mac An Ghaill, 1996). Power relations can be asymmetrical or symmetrical and this influences negotiations. Shuijing and Baibin encountered a good deal of asymmetrical negotiational contexts in their original families, their primary and secondary schools but it changed significantly in their narrative of early adulthood. Baibin tended to internalise the hegemonic prescriptive gender discourses with parents or peers and this became a criteria for his gender self-evaluation (Bandura, 1986; Egan and Perry, 2001).

Shuijing demonstrated a turning point in her gender self-acceptance in the teacher education institution. An expanded social circle allowed her to see a different range of gender attributes. Her feelings of being accepted as she was, in the Christian cell group enhanced her gender self-confidence. She could find cross-gender attributes in other men and women at college that fitted well within both sexes. Shuijing's narration of masculinity and femininity as being gender attributes at opposite ends of a continuum was challenged. It was un-learnt and she coined herself as being 'care free'—enjoying showing off her long legs in trousers as her uniquely feminine feature.

Learning has always been closely related to the media, through people, books and various ways of communication (Schmidt, 2010). Baibin did not appear to have as many opportunities as Shuijing to share his inner feelings and doubts with other people. His learning medium was more confined to books—here he felt assured his concept of masculinity and femininity was a blended beauty. The lack of conversation with oneself and others in a mutually trusting and interdependent relationship could have limited the political power of narration. Baibin's reflection on their participation in the life history, and focused group interviews, which facilitates second order observation (Schmidt, 2010), indicates the potential of narration as a vehicle for learning through gender renegotiation. In comparison to the individual interview, Baibin was able to talk much more about his father and analyse the family situations in the focus group interview.

> From these two interviews, individual and group—my perspectives broadened. I have two points to make. Firstly, I seldom talk about my life story because I'm sort of an introvert. I fulfilled my responsibility during the first interview because I had committed and agreed to join the project. Secondly I was rather interested in this topic. The process has allowed me to reflect on my own gender identity, my career and how the two interact. The discussion today stimulates a lot of thoughts in me which I would like to share (focus group).

Influence of cultural context   Gender identities are fashioned in social, historical and cultural contexts. The different situations of Shuijing and Baibin can be seen to reflect the changes in the wider social and cultural contexts in Hong Kong in two ways. Firstly, there was gender equity and equal opportunities for females emphasised more during Shuijing's early socialization. Secondly, there was the fact that the prescriptive hegemonic male image remained prominent in gender discourse in Hong Kong.

Shuijing's parents allowed her a choice of toys and to a certain extent, the choice of extra-curricular activities. On the other hand Baibin had less freedom to explore cross-gender choices that differed from the traditional cultural norm—as witnessed when his complexion and fear of insects made him the laughing stock of his family. His sense of inferiority 'as a true man' was further reinforced in both the context of his marital relations and his occupational position. This could probably be related to at least two reasons. Firstly, efforts to understand men's lives (body image, work, emotional disconnection and divorce) were only developed in mid 1990s, after the feminist movements of the late 70s to early 90s (Connell, 2000). If the 'boy's turn' in the research agenda is only a fairly recent interest, there is little doubt that stereotypical male roles remained hegemonic and hard to challenge (Weaver-Hightower, 2003).

Personal values, which have their cultural root, play a role in gender identity negotiations. Shuijing and Baibin have been holding onto certain traditional Chinese values such as filial piety and familism (Lau and Kuan, 1990; Luk-Fong, 2010). Baibin pushed himself to take up 'male role of responsibility' at 12 years old to look after his family. His love and empathy for his mother's situation further strengthened his internalisation to prescribed male roles. He put a lot of emphasis on masculine characteristics such as bravery, taking on responsibilities and he felt ashamed of being a coward in the face of challenges. Similarly, empathy with her mother also contributed to Shuijing's 'masculine' attributes such as being tough, not easily crying—so as not to worry her mother.

Shuijing and Baibin's lived experiences echo Inglehart and Baker's (2000) view that while there have been significant cultural changes in the process of modernisation—distinctive traditional values are remarkably durable and resilient. Thus gender identity negotiation not only involves the politics of narration, but also the evolution of a society's cultural contexts.

ACKNOWLEDGEMENTS

This chapter is one of the outcomes generated by the project 'Contemporary Chinese Teachers' Experiences of Changing Gender Identities: A Case Study of Secondary School Teachers in Hong Kong', funded by the Hong Kong Institute of Education.

REFERENCES

Archer, M. (1999). *Structure, agency and the internal conversation*. Cambridge: Cambridge University Press.

Bandura, A. (1986). The explanatory and predictive scope of self-efficacy theory. *Journal of Social and Clinical Psychology, 4*, 359–373.

Biklen, S. K. (1995). *School work. Gender and the cultural construction of teaching*. New York: Teachers College Press.

Casey, K. (1990). Teacher as mother: Curriculum theorizing in the life histories of contemporary women teachers. *Cambridge Journal of Education, 20*(3), 301–311.

Chan, A. K. (2004). Gender, school management and educational reforms: A case study of a primary school in Hong Kong. *Gender and Education, 16*, 491–500.

Cheung, F.M.(1986). Development of gender stereotype. *Educational Research Journal, 1*, 68–73.

Cheung, F.M., Lai, B. L. L., Au, K. C. & Ngai, S. S. H. (1997). Gender role identity, stereotypes and attitudes in Hong Kong. In F. M. Cheung (Ed.). *EnGendering Hong Kong society: A gender Perspective of women's status,* pp. 201–235. Hong Kong: The Chinese University of Hong Kong.

Chow, W. S. (2000). *Border-crossing of gender in China.* [In Chinese]. Hong Kong: Xianggang Tongzhi Yanjiu Shi.

Connell, R. W. (1996). Teaching the boys: New research on masculinity, and gender strategies for schools. *The Teachers College Record, 98*(6), 206–235.

Connell, R. W. (2000). *The men and the boys.* Berkeley, Calif: University of California Press.

Coffey, A., & Delamont, S. (2000). *Feminism and the classroom teacher. Research, praxis and pedagogy.* London and New York: Routledge.

Egan, S. K., & Perry, D. G. (2001). Gender identity: a multi-dimensional analysis with implications for psychosocial adjustment. *Developmental Psychology, 37*(4), 451–463.

Feng, L. C. (2011). *Boys all lose in tertiary education* [Chinese]. Xinbao, 21 April, 2011.

Goodson, I. F., Biesta, G. J. J., Tedder, M., & Adair, N. (2010). Narrative learning. London and New York: Routledge.

Goodson, I. F., & Choi, P. L. (2008). Life history and collective memory as methodological strategies: Studying teacher professionalism. *Teacher Education Quarterly, 35*(2), 5–28.

Goodson, I. F., & Sikes, P. (2001). *Life history research in educational settings: Learning from lives.* Buckingham: Open University.

Hall, S. (1990). Cultural identity and diaspora. In J. Rutherford (Ed.) *Identity, culture, difference,* 222–235. London: Lawrence & Wishart.

Hoffman, R. M. (2006). Self-definition and gender self-acceptance in women: Intersections with feminist, womanist and ethnic identities. *Journal of Counselling & Development, 84*(3), 58–72.

Inglehart, R., & Baker, W. E. (2000). Modernization, cultural change, and the persistence of traditional values. *American Sociological Review, 65*(1), 19–51.

Josselson, R. (2006). Narrative research and the challenge of accumulating knowledge. *Narrative Inquiry, 16*(1), 3–10.

Ko, D. (1994). *Teachers of the inner chambers: Women and culture in seventeenth-century China.* Stanford, CA: Stanford University Press.

Lau, S. K., & Kuan, H. C. (1988). *The ethos of Hong Kong Chinese.* Hong Kong: The Chinese University Press.

Leung, B. (1996). *Perspectives on Hong Kong society.* Hong Kong: Oxford University Press.

Lewin, M. (1984). 'Rather worse than folly?' Psychology measures femininity and masculinity. In M. Lewin (Ed.). In the shadow of the past: psychology portrays the sexes, pp. 155–178. New York: Columbia University Press.

Luk, B. (1981). Advocating for equal education opportunity for full development of potentials [In Chinese]. *Ming Palo Monthly Magazine, 16*(6), 41–44.

Luk-Fong, P. Y. Y. (2010). Towards a hybrid conceptualisation of Chinese women primary school teachers' changing femininities. A case study of Hong Kong. *Gender and Education, 22*(1), 73–86.

Mac an Ghaill, M. (1996). Deconstructing heterosexualities within school arenas. *Pedagogy, Culture & Society, 4*(2), 191–209.

Morgan, D. L. (1998). *The focus group guidebook.* Thousand Oaks, CA, Sage.

Moschella, M. (2006). Personal identity and gender. In *Gender identities in a globalised world.* New York: Humanity Books, 75–108.

Munro, P. (1998) *Subject to fiction: Women teachers' life history narratives and the cultural politics of resistance.* Buckingham, Open University Press.

Ossana, S. M., Helms, J. E., & Leonard, M. M. (1992). Do 'womanist' identity attitudes influence college women's self-esteem and perceptions of environmental bias? *Journal of Counselling & Development, 70,* 402–408.

Polkinghorne, Donald E. (2007). Validity issues in narrative research. *Qualitative Inquiry, 13*(4), 471–486.

Rebecca, M., Hefner, R., & Olenshansky, B. A. (1976). A model of sex-role transcendence. *Journal of Social Issues, 32,* 197–206.

Sabbe, E., & Aelterman, A. (2007). Gender in teaching: A literature review, *Teachers and Teaching, 13*(5), 521–538.

Schenk, C. E. (2008). Economic history of Hong Kong. In R. Whaples, *EH. Net Encyclopedia.* March 16, 2008. http://eh.net/encyclopedia/article/schenk.HongKong

Schmidt, S. (2010). Self-organization and learning culture. *Constructivist Foundations, 5*(3), 121–129.
Smedley, S. (2007). Learning to be a primary school teacher: reading one man's story, *Gender and Education, 19*(3), 369–385.
Spence, D. P. (1982). *Narrative truth and historical truth.* New York: Norton.
Tamboukou, M. (2000). The paradox of being a woman teacher, *Gender and Education, 12*(4), 463–478.
Wayne, M., & Blye, F. (2006). The tyranny of surveillance: male teachers and the policing of masculinities in a single sex school, *Gender and Education, 18*(1), 17–33.
Weaver-Hightower, M. (2003). The 'Boy Turn' in research on gender and education. *Review of Educational Research, 73*(4), 471–498.

AFFILIATION

Pik Lin Choi
Department of Education and Leadership,
Hong Kong Institute of Education

6. 'JUST BECAUSE I'M FROM AFRICA, THEY THINK I'LL WANT TO DO NARRATIVE'

Problematising Narrative Inquiry

INTRODUCTION

Narrative inquiry is undoubtedly a seductive methodological approach for many people, in particular because storytelling is a universal practice; the ways that stories are told and listened to—and those considered to be legitimate—differ, however, from place to place. All narratives are rooted in context and this rootedness has to be taken account of so that stories are interpreted according to the local knowledge of that context. We are troubled that many of our doctoral researchers who have rarely encountered qualitative research previously, let alone narrative, are using it in their research even though it is either totally unknown in their own context or, if it is known, is criticised for not being 'real research'. This raises ethical questions for us. By encouraging researchers to use narrative is this another form of colonialism? Should we rather be paying due care and attention to methodological approaches that might be more suitable, so called 'critical and indigenous methodologies' rather than supporting narrative inquiry? Or, even worse, might we be accused (falsely) of assuming that because a researcher is from an 'oral culture' then narrative is congruent with that culture and thus the researcher is ideally suited to use it? This chapter discusses these concerns, drawing on our experiences as researchers and doctoral supervisors. In the first part, we will focus upon three inter-connected areas that trouble us. First the relationship of the 'grand western narrative' of research to our work as international researchers and educators, second the relationship of narrative to research environments, settings or contexts, and third the issue of the 'translation' of research practices, particularly analytic models (intellectual, ideological and practical) from one setting to another. In the second part of the chapter we will examine issues around the promotion of narrative methods when working with graduate students from the south.

PART ONE: THE 'GRAND NARRATIVE', CONTEXT AND TRANSLATION

The 'Grand Narrative' in Educational Research

At the heart of an understanding of what constitutes narrative is the relationship between *what* is being told i.e. its content, *how* it is being narrated, i.e. its form, *for whom* it is intended, i.e. the audience, and *where* this narrating or enacting is

Ivor F. Goodson, Avril M. Loveless and David Stephens (Eds.), Explorations in Narrative Research, 59–70.

occurring, i.e. the context. Narrative is therefore composed of a dialectical relationship between knowledge, audience and context. In the West the relationship between these three component parts has been shaped by what Lyotard (1984) has termed the 'grand narrative'.

This is not the place to debate the merits or otherwise of post-modernism, but rather to examine the extent to which the concept of a 'grand narrative' helps us understand the nature of western and non-western interpretations of what constitutes knowledge and, in turn, the extent to which western forms of knowledge are in fact as shaped by cultural and contextual forces as much as non-western ones are. Knowledge and narratives are therefore not universal, but as Odora Hoppers (2002) states, *knowledges* or ideological world views seek both to explain and legitimate understandings and conceptions of the world.

A starting point is Lyotard's idea of 'grand narrative' (1984) which takes issue with the established 'totalising nature of meta-narratives' or 'universal essential truths'. The problem of the 'grand narrative' as a concept is the de-linking or de-contextualizing of knowledge from its context or culture under the pretext of its universality. In fact there is much evidence to support the idea that Lyotard's 'grand narrative' is in fact an epistemological view of knowledge shaped by the twin forces of context and culture, and in particular power, colonialism, language and rationality. All narratives, whether 'grand' or otherwise, we would argue derive from context and culture.

Lyotard (1984) refers to what he describes as the postmodern condition, which he characterises as increasing scepticism towards the totalising nature of 'meta-narratives' or grand narratives typically characterised by some form of 'transcendent and universal truth'.

If there is indeed no single meta-narrative through which to explain the world, this is not to deny the power of narrative in advancing knowledge of ourselves and the world.

One of the most influential writers on the potential for narrative in advancing knowledge is the psychologist Jerome Bruner.

It is through our own narratives that we principally construct a version of ourselves in the world and it is through its narrative that a culture provides modes of identity and agency to its members (1996, p. 15).

In two of the most important chapters of *The Culture of Education 'Narratives of Science' and The Narrative Construal of Reality*—Bruner argues against one all-encompassing explanatory meta-narrative—and he has Sigmund Freud and Jean Piaget in mind here—instead making the case for 'universals of narrative realities' which are themselves given meaning when grounded in 'cultural and historical circumstances' (1996, p. 135). These universals, for example, 'a structure of committed time', 'inherent negotiability', and 'hermeneutic composition' provide the heuristic linkage between the psychological 'inner' world of the learner with the external world of society and culture.

For Bruner it is the super-organic characteristic or quality of culture that connects the individual story to the broader social narrative. As he says,

Culture... assigns meanings to things in different settings on particular occasions. Meaning making involves situating encounters within the world in their appropriate cultural contexts in order to know what they are about. Although meanings are 'in the mind', they have their origins and their significance in the culture in which they are created. It is the cultural situatedness of meanings that assures their negotiability, and ultimately, their communicability (1996, p. 3).

At the heart of problematising narrative inquiry therefore is the role of narrative, with its universal strength and recognition, in providing a bridge, between individual and social meanings. These meanings, however, are only meaningful in relation to particular circumstances grounded in more general situations.

Context Matters

Narrative and narrative knowledge or knowing therefore gains meaning when understood in terms of the context or situation in which it is generated, and importantly when employed in a variety of different cultural settings.

In one of our recent books (Stephens, 2009) we have argued that despite the advances in qualitative research methodology there is still a tendency to view 'context' as a backdrop or background to the research enquiry and that this background needs to be fore-grounded for any narratives generated to be meaningful.

Naomi Scheman (2011, p. 1) expresses it well when she says, 'At its most fundamental, narrative and narrative saliency constitute the ontology of complex objects as more than the sum of their parts'.

The suggestion is that context or foreground provides the essential epistemological 'glue' that binds together the component parts of a narrative. Let's think for a moment what these 'parts' consist of: the object and subject of the research (researcher and researched), the cultural context of the enquiry, and the language in which the research is being conducted are some. But what seems of central significance is not just the 'objects' of the narrative inquiry but the prior interpretations the researcher *and* the reader brings to that inquiry.

As Roy Dilley says (Dilley, 1998) context is, intrinsically connected to matters of meaning and on-going interpretation. It is about making connections and, by implication, dis-connections: contexts being sets of connections construed as relevant to someone, to something or to a particular problem, this process, 'yielding an explanation, a sense, an interpretation for the object so connected' (Dilley, 1998).

Paraphrasing the great philosopher Wittgenstein, Dilley suggests we focus less on what context 'means' and more on how it is 'used'. Context can indeed be used to help frame the research problem. It can also be used in theory as well as in practice, connecting (or disconnecting) us to ideas and concepts across a range of academic and professional disciplines. Perhaps we can apply the same approach to narrative research? We would go even further and suggest that building connections in a constructivist sense between the constituent parts of the narrative is actually more useful than establishing a research question and then looking for an answer. This construction draws heavily upon hermeneutics.

The relationship of the part to the whole—or the 'hermeneutic circle'—is central to an understanding of the relationship of context, interpretation and narrative. Or rather what matters is that the process of interpretation occurs in context: research findings or 'new knowledge' being initially interpreted in the context from which they derive; the findings then allowing for a subsequent re-interpretation of that context in the light of the analysis of the data. Interpretation and context are key players in the dramatic story unfolding during the research project. They shape not only the content of the research but, we would argue, the methodological tools used in the research process. For example, Andrews, Squire and Tamboukou (2011, p. 24) in writing about how they 'teach' narrative inquiry to students from all over the world highlight how,

> Conventional Aristotelian notions of narrative genres such as tragedy and comedy get disturbed by participants with quite different canonic story genres: western ideas about the centrality of self-narratives to individual lives are put in question by participants from the global South, in particular for whom more collectively framed narratives are often much more important in their research.

Lost in Translation

Our third area of discussion concerns the uncritical translation of ideas, such as 'narrative methodology' from one cultural setting to another.

Linda Tuhiwai Smith (1999) argues that all research involves a constant interchange between the scholarly and the imaginative construction of ideas about the 'other' (Said, 1999). This is particularly so when researchers from the west work with 'others' in the south.

The movement of ideas from west to south is now pronounced and hastened by the forces of globalisation. Appadurai (1996) refers to 'cultural flows' such as what he terms 'ideoscapes', the movement between west and south of political ideologies derived from Euro-American Enlightenment world-views.

The changing global landscape in which the narrative researcher is working is now a contested one in which both western and indigenous researchers working from and in the south are beginning to address questions of 'self-determination, decolonization and social justice' (Tuhiwai Smith, 1999, p.4). Narrative inquiry, in other words, like any other form of inquiry is not an ideologically neutral endeavour but one suffused with issues of ideology, positioning and purpose.

Specifically in terms of the development of narrative analysis, Cortazzi (1993, p. 101) reminds us that,

> Narrative… is a discourse structure or genre which reflects culture. It is central medium of cultural expression, organisation and learning. Furthermore it also creates cultural contexts.

This has resonance for the promotion of narrative as both a methodology and method, particularly when used in a variety of cultural settings.

Cortazzi (1993) goes on to make the point that there exists a 'range of cultural variation in the internal structure and function of narrative' (1993, p. 107). Such variation includes the structure of the narrative, function, performance and the role of the audience in performance.

There are also important relationships between narrative and knowledge (the epistemological function) and research purposes of narrative in relation to the broad aims of the inquiry. As much as setting and context are important in understanding the meaning to be derived from narrative, so is the relationship between the researcher or researcher-narrator and the researched or researched-narrator. Such a relationship, like that between supervisor and student, is redolent with issues of power, gender and status.

As Cortazzi (1993) notes, the race, age, gender, social and cultural background and so on, of the researcher, and the relationship between them must be accounted for.

In problematising narrative inquiry we are arguing, therefore, for attention to be paid to matters of traditions—western and non-western, positionality—that of the researcher and researched and context in both the defining of narrative and its use as an effective and innovative method of enquiry.

In the second part we will examine in further detail how the concerns we have raised so far are played out in the research supervisor-student relationship.

PART TWO: THE RESEARCH STUDENT-SUPERVISOR RELATIONSHIP

Denzin and Lincoln (2008, p. 6) refer to 'narrative, performative methodologies' as being 'reflexively consequential, ethical, critical, respectful and humble'. Reading Denzin and Lincoln's words, we might legitimately draw parallels with the fundamental principles of narrative inquiry that we both espouse—that it should be reflexive, critical and respectful—and by respectful we mean that it should pay due care and attention to the context within which it is situated. But, when working with doctoral researchers, no matter how much we might seek to work collaboratively with them and resist the power that might be ascribed to us as supervisors, the researcher is looking to us for guidance, certainly in the early days of their doctoral journey Perhaps it is inevitable, therefore, that, they will espouse a methodological approach that we favour. Our concern is not that they espouse the approach, more that they do so mindfully and that they critique its value within their own context. One reason why we are so drawn to narrative inquiry is because it does not privilege one dominant way of knowing; we consider it to be particularly appropriate, therefore, in the type of cross-cultural research that we do. Similarly, Andrews (2007, p. 489) advocates narrative enquiry in cross-cultural research because of the importance of 'being able to imagine a world other than the one we know... the seeing of difference' is crucial. It is challenging, however, to imagine worlds other than those that we believe we 'know'; the seeing of 'difference' is more complex and, in addition:

> Power struggles within ethnicity, class, caste, religious orientation, disabilities, skin color, nationality and immigration all have one common denominator—the focus on difference... this attention to difference is global and pervasive. We agree that this attention to difference is mostly evocative of negative thoughts and emotions. We agree that difference is highlighted or created by those with more power to justify privilege and subjugation. (Diversi and Moreira, 2009, p. 220)

By accident of birth, we fall into that group that has 'more power to justify privilege and subjugation' yet we resist, vigorously such privilege and power that may be ascribed to us and that we have done nothing to deserve. Diversi and Moreira, challenge those they describe as 'self-proclaimed resistance scholars declaring to value lived experience while in the same breath continuing to privilege Foucaultian analysis of power over pedestrian narratives of blood and profanity' (ibid, p. 33). Maybe this is what troubles us. We position ourselves as 'resistance scholars', resistant to what we perceive to be continuing dominant discourses in academia, in both research and in teaching (Trahar, 2011) yet, throughout this chapter and to some extent with our doctoral researchers, we continue to privilege theorising, possibly to a lesser extent than many, but nonetheless, we do so.

'Indigenous'? 'Non-indigenous'?

The word 'indigenous' is almost never applied to those researching in 'western' or 'northern' contexts; researching life in an English village, for example, would not be termed 'indigenous research' whereas doing similar research in Africa would (Trahar, 2011). When Denzin and Lincoln (2008, p. 11) assert,

> Indigenists deploy... interpretive strategies and skills fitted to the needs, language and traditions of their respective indigenous community. These strategies emphasise personal performance narratives and *tesimonios.*

We infer that we are not included in their definition yet, Tedlock (2000 cited Tomaselli, Dyll and Francis, 2008, p. 351) distinguishes between an indigenous researcher, that is anyone researching their own communities and a 'native ethnographer' who has 'their origins in non-European or non-western cultures and who share(s) a history of colonialism or an economic relationship based upon subordination'. Irrespective of these attempts to distinguish between terms, our view is that the word 'indigenous' is rarely used to describe people like us—white, westerners. By encouraging 'indigenist researchers' to use narrative, are we then behaving as the critical pedagogues that we position ourselves as? In other words are we, as non-indigensists behaving mindfully and respectfully by encouraging our doctoral researchers to honour their own local knowledge and to develop their methodological approach so that it is fully grounded in their own local context?

Another fear that we share is that narrative enquiry will join the 'canonical hegemony' and become another form of 'paradigm fundamentalism' (ibid, p. 357) unless we problematise its use and application. Perhaps terms such as canonical hegemony and paradigm fundamentalism summarise our concern: that rather than support and encourage all researchers to develop methodological approaches that are grounded in their local contexts and that pay attention to the ways in which knowledge is shared and understood in those contexts, we are privileging a methodological approach that we consider to be suited to those contexts. Because of the power that doctoral researchers may ascribe to us they may find our propositions difficult to challenge. But, if we take that position then we are assuming that our doctoral researchers are without agency—which is deeply patronising, 'they' also have the power to draw the line around us' (ibid, p. 364.)

Perhaps a fundamental question to ask at this stage is 'What *does* narrative inquiry help us to learn about our phenomenon that other theories or methods do not' (Clandinin and Connelly, 2000, p. 123, original emphasis)? A quality of narrative inquiry that differentiates it from many other qualitative methodological approaches is that experience, rather than theoretically informed research questions about that experience, is the starting point (Phillion and He, 2008). This does not mean that narrative inquirers eschew theory, more that they believe that people do not always 'fit' the theory and that '(western) theoretical constructs and ethical stipulations are not metaphysical ends or sets of values in their own right. They must always be open to re-examination and change' (Tomaselli, Dyll and Francis, 2008, p. 350). As indicated earlier in this chapter, narrative inquiry is informed by a range of philosophical perspectives, in particular, interpretivism and social constructionism but it also 'bumps up against post-positivism, Marxism and post-structuralism' (Clandinin and Rosiek, 2007, p. 59). Although 'narrative inquirers frequently find themselves crossing cultural discourses, ideologies and institutional boundaries' (ibid), these cultural discourses and ideologies remain rooted firmly in European thought, one of our main concerns as indicated earlier and that we are seeking to explore in this chapter.

We contend, however, that, in addition to its not being theory driven, a great strength of narrative inquiry is that it enables readers to see transparently how interactions between researcher and research participants help to shape and structure research texts. Through such transparency, we are thus able to glimpse— and sometimes more than glimpse—the larger historical, social and cultural stories within which we all dwell and that inform the stories that we tell and how we tell them. 'Stories don't fall from the sky (or emerge from the innermost 'self'), they are composed and received in contexts—interactional, historical, institutional and discursive—to name a few' (Riessman, 2008, p. 105). So the stories that research participants tell to researchers can never be unmediated or stories created only through their interaction in a particular context and in a particular relationship. They are stories formed and informed by the wider historical, social and cultural contexts and, provided that we are transparent about this, perhaps the discourses that dominate narrative inquiry lose their hegemony?

Working with Doctoral Researchers

We both work in Schools of Education with an increasing number of international students. One of us, Sheila Trahar, also works in a Graduate School of Education with an international reputation for narrative inquiry—many people come to the School to undertake the Doctor of Education in Narrative Inquiry or to carry out Ph.D. research because of that reputation—and so it is inevitable that many doctoral researchers will be influenced by that approach. In addition, as the supervisor then, much as Sheila might struggle to encourage researchers to take approaches that 'fit' with them and with their topic, perhaps there is an inevitability that they will want to use a methodological approach which not only attracts them because it is often very different from ways in which they have conducted research previously, but because they know that she favours it. Her stirrings of discomfort began in 2007 when a researcher from Cyprus was required to provide a set of interview questions to the Ministry of Education in order to gain permission to do her research in Cypriot primary schools. She struggled to explain that her methodological approach of narrative inquiry did not involve structured or even semi-structured interviews. In the end, supervisor and student decided that she would need to compromise in order to gain the permission that she needed and provide a set of questions that would probably never be asked. As the research progressed, she told Sheila that she had decided to use a diluted form of narrative inquiry, as she feared that embracing this methodological approach fully; in ways that she perceived others doing would render her research less credible in Cyprus.

Sheila recalls challenging a Malaysian doctoral researcher to reflect on the appropriateness of some of the philosophical ideas that inform narrative, such as post-modernism, social constructionism, post-structuralism, critical theory and to consider how those ideas sat within her context and, more importantly, with her Islamic faith. This challenge resulted in the researcher being much more questioning of these philosophical concepts and their relevance within her world rather than simply accepting them as western hegemonic truths. Such conversations encourage researchers to reflect more critically but there remains a conundrum. We may make glib assumptions that because people are from 'oral cultures' they will be more attracted to narrative, as if it were irrelevant that the context from which they came privileged more positivist paradigms. The words that form part of the title of this chapter were not spoken about either of us but they reflect those concerns. Are we behaving unethically by supporting people to use this approach? They are the ones who need to explain its rationale in their context, a context that is, more often than not, unimpressed by the value of qualitative research, let alone a methodological approach that involves the researcher in intense reflexivity.

More recently, a doctoral researcher from Ghana, nearing the end of her Ph.D. journey, writes of how, for her as a member of the Akan people, storytelling continues to be integral as a form of education. Encountering narrative inquiry, during her research training programme at Bristol, she was sceptical that she could use this very familiar form to conduct her research. Knowing that it would be 'revolutionary' in her context, nonetheless she decided to use it. But, she was distraught at the ways in which her participants responded to her narrative interviewing style. Sharing her own experiences where they resonated with those of her narrators did not 'unlock the pouring out of stories' rather her participants positioned her as in need of their support; they judged her as being inadequate and a victim. She often emerged from interviews feeling that she had been 'unprepared in their eyes'. Sheila began to read in her draft chapters of how she was influenced by African scholars who admonish African researchers for using, unquestioningly, western conceptual schemes of knowledge and theories in their scholarship, considering this to be another form of colonialism. Sheila had written about those very issues herself; she had discussed them with her, encouraging her to mount a critique of narrative interviewing in her dissertation Yet, it was not until she communicated this strength of feeling to her through her writing that a space was opened up for both of them to have more fruitful and robust conversations about such complexities. It seemed that, reading that others from her context were raising similar questions to her supervisor, gave her questioning more credibility and she found the confidence to be more questioning in her own writing. To Sheila's delight, her final doctoral thesis is therefore woven throughout with poems, verbatim theatre and visual images of Ghanaian tribal cloths to represent local myths and stories. The dissertation has to be presented in English, but occasionally she writes in her own language. Tiring of being asked to explain the theoretical basis of her work whenever she presented it, she found the courage to challenge that western academic convention by including fictionalised emails from her parents in which they were her 'academic voices', reminding her how their tribal stories informed her understanding of the world.

CONCLUSION

So—after having lain bare our anxieties and presented what we consider to be plausible arguments for the use of narrative inquiry in different contexts—our question is 'Were we worrying unnecessarily'? We do not believe so because through our worrying we have created space to articulate these concerns. Provided that we encourage doctoral researchers who are captivated by narrative to investigate how others from their context have used it, in so far as that is possible, or how others from post-colonial contexts have used narrative then we consider that we are behaving mindfully and ethically. Maybe through our deliberations what we have created is a liminal space, a 'betweener' space and so we conclude our chapter with extracts from a poem used by the Brazilian writers Diversi and Moreira (2009, p. 223) to end their performance text 'Betweener Talk: Decolonizing Knowledge Production, Pedagogy and Praxis':

We are all betweeners
Us, betweeners,
Them, betweeners
You, betweener
We are
Not ready to settle

Willing to struggle for a world without Them
Where everybody is
And should be
Us

Provided that 'Us' does not lead to what Manathunga (2007) refers to as a 'liberal *disavowal of difference'* (p. 95, original emphasis) in which people feel that their 'difference' is not acknowledged thus rendering 'them' silent, then we are pleased to place ourselves as ' Us, betweeners'.

REFERENCES

Andrews, M. (2007). Exploring cross-cultural boundaries. In D. J. Clandin (Ed.) *Handbook of narrative inquiry*, 489–511. Thousand Oaks, Ca: Sage.
Andrews, M., Squire, C., & Tamboukou, M. (2011). Interfaces in teaching narratives. In S. Trahar (Ed.) *The learning and teaching of narrative inquiry: Travelling in the borderlands*, 15–32. Amsterdam: John Benjamins.
Appadurai, A. (1996). *Modernity at large: Cultural dimensions of globalisation.* Minneapolis: University of Minneapolis.
Bruner, J. (1996). *The culture of education.* Cambridge, Mass: Harvard University Press.
Clandinin, D. J., & Connelly, F. M. (2000). *Narrative inquiry: Experience and story in qualitative research.* San Francisco, Ca: Jossey-Bass.
Clandinin, D. J., & Roziek, J. (2007). Mapping a landscape of narrative inquiry: Borderland spaces and tensions. In D. J. Clandin (Ed.) *Handbook of narrative inquiry mapping a methodology*, 35–75. Thousand Oaks, Ca: Sage.
Cortazzi, M. (1993). *Narrative analysis.* London: Falmer Press.
Denzin, N. K., & Lincoln, Y. S. (2008). Introduction: Critical methodologies and indigenous inquiry. In N. K. Denzin, Y. S. Lincoln & L. Tuhiwai Smith, (Eds.) *Handbook of critical and indigenous methodologies*, 1–20. Thousand Oaks, Ca: Sage.
Dilley, R. (1998). *The problem of context.* New York: Berghahn Books.
Diversi, M., & Moreira, C. (2009). *Betweener talk: decolonizing knowledge production, pedagogy ad praxis.* Walnut Creek, Ca: Left Coast Press.
Lyotard, J. F. (1984). *The post-modern condition: A report on knowledge.* Minnesota: University of Minnesota Press.
Manathunga, C. (2007). Intercultural postgraduate supervision: Ethnographic journeys of identity and power. In D. Palfreyman & D. L. McBride (Eds.) *Learning and teaching across cultures in higher education*, 93–113. Basingstoke: Palgrave Macmillan.
Odora Hoppers, C. (2002). *Indigenous knowledge and the integration of knowledge systems: Towards a philosophy of articulation.* South Africa: New Africa Books.
Phillion, J., & He, M. F. (2008). Multicultural and cross-cultural narrative inquiry in educational research. *Thresholds in education*, XXXIV, (1 & 2), 2–12.
Riessman, C. K. (2008). *Narrative methods for the human sciences.* Thousand Oaks, Ca: Sage.
Said, E (1999). *Orientalism*, New York: Vintage Books.
Scheman, N. (2011). *Narrative, complexity, and context: Autonomy as an epistemic value* (forthcoming). In H. Lindemann & M. Verkerk (Eds.) Naturalized bio-ethics: Towards responsible knowing and practice. Cambridge: Cambridge University Press.
Stephens, D. (2009). *Qualitative research in international settings: A practical guide.* London and New York: Routledge.
Tomaselli, K. G., Dyll, L., & Francis, M. (2008). 'Self' and 'other': Auto-reflexive and indigenous ethnography. In N. K. Denzin, Y. S. Lincoln & L. Tuhiwai Smiyh (Eds.) *Handbook of critical and indigenous methodologies*, 347–372. Thousand Oaks, Ca: Sage.

Trahar, S. (2011). *Developing cultural capability in international higher education: A narrative inquiry.* London: Routledge.
Tuhiwai Smith, L. (1999). *Decolonizing methodologies: Research and indigenous peoples.* London: Zed Books.

AFFILIATIONS

David Stephens
Education Research Centre,
University of Brighton

Sheila Trahar
Graduate School of Education,
University of Bristol

HÅKAN LÖFGREN

7. QUESTIONING THE NARRATIVE OF MORE MALE TEACHERS AS THE EASY SOLUTION TO PROBLEMS IN SWEDISH SCHOOLS

'A MAN'S GOT TO DO WHAT A MAN'S GOT TO DO' [1]

The aim of this chapter is to investigate how life history methods can contribute to the discussion of gender in school. More specifically, teachers' stories form the basis of a critical discussion of the Swedish government's use of the concepts, 'traditional gender roles' and 'male role models'.

The Swedish government is concerned by discipline problems and poor results in secondary education. Comparing results with other countries investigated in the PISA and TIMMS reports,[2] the government concludes that there is a 'crisis in the Swedish school' (Björklund, 2008a and 2008b). The rhetoric of an 'almost permanent "crisis"' (Ball, 2007, p. 5) in school is well known in other countries (Apple, 2006), as is the tendency to use concepts of gender for describing the problems and solutions (Arnesen et al., 2008). Male teachers are historically a politically important issue in the context of the Swedish welfare system where they have been considered to be 'The spearhead of gender equality' (Nordberg, 2005, p. 375). But the number of male teachers has fallen in Sweden and elsewhere in western countries. In 1985, 32 percent of the primary school teachers in Sweden were men and in 2010 the rate had fallen to 25 percent (SCB, 1985; Skolverket, 2011). This decrease has been used in government rhetoric, linking the lack of men in school with boys' failures with the emergence of an 'anti-swat-culture' (Björklund and Sabuni, 2008) among boys in school. Therefore, the National Agency for Higher Education has been mandated to initiate a campaign to recruit more male students to teacher education as a solution to the problem. In this chapter I discuss both the logic and the validity of this line of reasoning. The main issue so far, as I would argue, is not the number of male teachers in school, but what qualities men are supposed to contribute to the school environment. My argument is based on empirical data derived from a life history survey illustrating how gender is shaped when teachers tell their stories about a group of male teachers in the past.

THE GOVERNMENT NARRATIVE OF TOO FEW MALE TEACHERS

In a newspaper article, written by the Minister of Education, Jan Björklund, and the Minister for Gender Equality, Nyamko Sabuni, (2008), the plot of a gendered narrative in the school crisis and its solution is neatly summarised. The Ministers refer to an article in *The Economist* where Sweden is highlighted as a pioneer in creating equality between the sexes because of their equal performance in mathematics. They are not proud, however, because they claim that the similarity in achievement is a result of the boys' falling performance rather than the girls' rising performance. They continue as follows,

> Equal results are good, but the goal cannot be that everybody learns equally less. On the contrary, we need to raise the girls' results in Mathematics to the same high level that the boys once reached. And we have to make the boys perform better in school in general. There is also a need for more men in school, who can serve as role models for the boys (Björklund and Sabuni, 2008) (My translation).

In this statement they define sex as a major aspect to focus on when trying to improve results in Swedish schools. At a first glance, the governments' narrative about the crises and the suggested solution to employ more male teachers seem reasonable. But let us qualify the narrative and explore the details.

The Ministers' narrative goes like this—the source of the problems in school lies in the differences between the sexes in school. The boys are developing an 'anti-swat-culture' and they 'underperform' greatly in almost all school subjects. The girls' performance is better in most respects, but they have to face a school environment where insulting language is an everyday occurrence and psychological illness is spreading. An important problem, according to the Ministers, is that the adults in school fail to speak up clearly and if this continues, we will have 'the rowdiest classrooms in the world' and will fail to create 'the best school in Europe' (Björklund and Sabuni, 2008). Most teachers, that is, the adults in school, are women, the ministers note. The narrative so far is obviously not unique. Weak performance in national school systems has been emphasised for different reasons for a long time. It has been considered a major hindrance for producing skilled workers and citizens competing on a global market (Green, 2006). It is also at the heart of the neo-liberal construction of a crisis in school, which calls for new solutions and new (private) actors (Ball, 2007). The development of boys' subcultures challenging school has been discussed since Willis (1977) published his book *Learning to Labour*. And the issue of underperforming boys has been described as a 'travelling discourse' (Arnesen et al., 2008) coming to Sweden from Anglo-Saxon research and politics.

But some of the solutions to the problems have a national character, with origins in the gender equality discourses related to the Swedish welfare model. The first solution suggested by the government was to attract more male students to teacher education. These men were later supposed to serve as 'male role models' for the boys in schools. The Swedish National Agency for Higher Education was asked to inquire how to counteract the segregation in teacher education (Högskoleverket, 2009). A second solution was to introduce training for teachers on how to 'counteract traditional gender roles' (Björklund and Sabuni, 2008; Högskoleverket, 2009). Furthermore, the government allocated resources to counteract violence conditioned by cultures of honour and repression and expressed an ambition to improve teaching about sex and relationships.

In sum, the plot of the Government narrative goes like this—boys are causing trouble in school and girls are disturbed, so all students underachieve. Therefore, we need more male teachers so the boys have good 'role models' and stop causing trouble, and performance will improve. At the same time, teachers are expected to 'counteract traditional gender roles' by providing male role models for the boys as well as increasing their awareness of how to avoid traditional gender roles. These two strategies are incompatible, however, because there is an unsettling contradiction in claiming that men as culturally conditioned creatures have certain qualities that boys need to experience, while arguing that we need to counteract traditional gender roles. For, if we already know what a male role model is, it is by definition a traditional gender role and should, as the argument goes, be rejected. The role models, as they take shape in the ministers' rhetoric, are stereotypical constructions linked to the narrative of disciplining boys in order to improve school results and national competitiveness. But, historically, constructions of role models in Sweden have been framed by discourses of equality, questioning the gendered norms in school (Nordberg, 2005). Therefore, it is necessary to discuss what dimensions men are supposed to bring as role models in school and how traditional gender roles are (re-)shaped. At its best, narrative research can bring more nuances and complexities to that discussion. The concept of role models can be used as an incitement to change as well as to preserve traditional gender constructions.

GENDER EQUALITY DISCOURSES IN THE WELFARE STATE

It has been suggested that three different discourses of gender equality have dominated the debate in Sweden since the 70s (Nordberg, 2005). In the first, similarities between the sexes were emphasised. The issue of male schoolteachers as role models was frequently discussed in official documents and public debate. The dominant discourse of that time has been described as transgender equality where the similarities between the sexes were in focus, and men were supposed to do the same things as women do (Nordberg, 2005). Male teachers were supposed to renounce the 'harmful masculinity' characterised by authoritarian and competitive features. Later these male ideals were ridiculed.

The second discourse was influenced by the women's rights movement and differences between the sexes were emphasised. The struggle against patriarchal domination was central and women's culturally disposed position as subordinate drew attention to similarities between women. The 'female perspectives' (ibid, p. 85) was a means to open up male bastions. Finally, a third discourse gained ground in the 90s. Once again the differences between the sexes were emphasised, but this time it was not a means for changing power relations in society. The differences were now described as something positive and both men and women were seen as carriers of culturally predisposed, valuable assets. Women were stereotypically defined as emotional, responsive and socially skilled, while men were described as rational and action-oriented (Nordberg, 2005). The male role model that took shape out of a combination of these discourses by the end of the 90s have been thus described,

A male and patriarchically rooted head of the household with the task to rule over and foster the members of the household by a combination of caring and authority, and to inaugurate the boys of the family in male tasks and a male community. (Nordberg, 2005, p. 90) (My translation)

Voices from the Professionals

Instead of implying a nostalgic and general picture of strict male teachers associated with order in school, as is often done in the political rhetoric, we need to have specific and concrete illustrations from school contexts where people meet face to face as a point of departure for the discussion of how gender is shaped in school. Since the teachers are those required to counteract the 'traditional gender roles', their stories about male teachers now and in the past should be in focus. And if we want to catch nuances in teachers' views on men as role models in school, the life history method is appropriate (Goodson and Sikes, 2001). By trying to capture and analyse teachers 'collective memories' (Plummer, 2006, p. 235; Goodson and Choi, 2008), we can get a hint of how fragments of discourses and historical contexts 'haunt' (Freeman, 2010, p. 108) the teachers when they form their views on male teachers in their life stories today.

Viewing gender as a social construction (Connell, 1995) has consequences for data construction. Historical and relational aspects cannot be ignored. In my project, I conducted 15 individual life history interviews (Goodson and Sikes, 2001; Pérez Prieto, 2006) with eight teachers, four men and four women, who had been working at a secondary school, which was closed in 2007. When selecting participants, I considered differences in age, number of years in school and teaching subjects to encourage a rich variety of stories. The teachers' common background in the same school enabled me to analyse the socially situated gender constructions and changes over time. The interviews were conducted during, and immediately after, the closing of the school, which emphasised the historical moment and stimulated narrative reflection (Freeman, 2010). The teachers told of their own work as teachers and about the school now and in the past. When analysing the data, I found that all teachers told three stories about the school's past. I learned from Linde (2009) that stories that are known to all members of an institution and are 'retold' by members who were not present when the action took place are of special significance both to the institution and to the teller of the story. I borrow the term institutional memory (Linde, 2009) for this kind of stories. One of the three institutional memories in the data was about a group of strict and humorous men who once had a strong influence on the school. This institutional memory is imbued with notions of what a male teacher should be, and when the teachers tell their versions, they also take a stand on what they think. First I will present a short version of the institutional memory of the strict men and then I will continue with three different teachers' versions of the institutional memory to illustrate how gender is constructed in school narratives.

The Institutional Memory of the Strict Men in Lake School[3]

The Lake school opened in 1965 in a newly built residential area in the period of the 'Million Program'[4], which was a welfare project aiming to build one million new homes in ten years to eliminate the overcrowded and unhealthy houses in town centres in Sweden. When the teachers were recruited, a group of male teachers were 'handpicked' by the assistant headmaster, according to the teachers. The teachers say that these men knew each other before they were employed and that they shared a common interest in sports. They seem to have formed an informal inner circle at the school for about years, and socialising in their leisure and together with their families. They had close relations with the headmaster's office, but they were sceptical of external experts and influences. Two distinct features characterise these men as they take shape in the institutional memory. First, the interviewees describe them as 'strict'—sometimes they use the word 'strong/powerful'—in their contact with the students. They knew what was happening in the school and dealt with discipline problems immediately and resolutely. The interviewees talk about their abilities to 'chide' in an effective way, so there was no need for long procedures to maintain order in school. Secondly, these men are also described as humorous. The interviewees describe their verbal skills when telling a good story, and they describe in detail how they played different practical jokes on each other and others in school. The humour seems to have been of a daring kind and over the years they developed their own jargon, which is described as both including and excluding. They gladly joked about documents trying to introduce new pedagogical ideas, but the interviewees also mention how they humiliated students in the staff common room.

In the institutional memory of the strict men, the different storytellers give the male teachers different epithets indicating the different standpoints that the tellers take to their stories. The men are, for example, called 'strict and strong', 'the handpicked', 'individuals', 'knowledgeable', 'originals' and 'odd individuals'. A similarity between the epithets that are attributed to these men is that they tend to be described as confident, free or independent and as original personalities. In the institutional memory they stand out as persons who could say or do almost whatever they liked. In the following, I will consider the attitudes taken to the past by the interviewees in their stories about the men, talking about them in the twenty-first century.

Different Attitudes to the Institutional Memory of the Strict Men

The interviewees take mainly three different attitudes to the institutional memory of the strict men and here these are illustrated in the stories told by three of the interviewees. The first attitude is characterised by a kind of sorrow for the lost happy days, but also an insight that these days have really passed. Hedvig's story is a good illustration of this standpoint.

Hedvig began to work at Lake School in the fall of 1974 and she had just retired when I interviewed her. Her story begins with her first visit to the school just before the summer break. She thought it would be a good idea to visit the school to meet the headmaster and maybe some colleagues. After her meeting with the headmaster, she went to the staff common room, but there were only two people present—two men. One of them was about her own age—28, and the other a few years older. She mustered up courage and stepped forward and introduced herself:

Hedvig... and they started to poke fun at me so I both blushed and went white. And as I said, when I left, I was thinking, should I work at that madhouse? [Håkan: Ok ([Laughing] They didn't say a sensible word but were just joking, and so on. Yes, yes. Then I realised pretty soon that it suited me just fine (2008-10-22).

After this introduction she started to work at the school and she stayed at the same school for her whole career which she has never regretted. Of the interviewees, she is the one who most often refers back to stories about the strict men. Her stories about them always have positive overtones, which make them interesting in regard to defining the constructions of male teachers as role models and of gender roles in school. So the main question is—why did she like the male teachers?

One striking component is their sense of humour. She had fun in their company. She frequently uses expressions indicating that she felt really included by the jargon, e.g. 'I was about as crazy as they were'. She talks about the relaxed atmosphere in breaktime and how they talked about everything except school related problems in the staff common room. She implies that her company with the men gave her a reputation as a humorous person, and she says that she used humour in the classroom. She also says that she is aware that not everybody felt included by the jargon, but she didn't mind if they made jokes about her dresses. Still, she wouldn't be surprised if other women teachers thought differently.

Hedvig: They (other women), sort of, thought that they were biased hi-men [Håkan: Yes.] with elements of sexism and a bit of oppressive mentality towards girls and so on—it wouldn't surprise me. [Håkan: No.] It wouldn't. [Håkan: No, no.] But I would lie if I said that was my experience. [—] I thought they were a support to me who came there [Håkan: Yes.] tiny and trivial and young and... yes (2008-10-22).

Even if I can sense a streak of irony in the last comment, Hedvig stands out as a person one would hardly call 'trivial'. Nevertheless, the last comment spells out the second component of what she liked about the male teachers—namely the informal supportive side. She says that there was a spirit during these first years in which the colleagues 'stood up' for each other. She exemplifies this with a story of a boy who had done something 'really stupid' in a lesson in home economics. One of the strict men immediately gathered all the teachers together who knew the boy, into the library and they told him what they thought of his behaviour. After that he 'became really good'. The interesting features of this story are that the teachers stuck together, that they reacted immediately and that the process was short. A final point that Hedvig makes in her stories is that the male teachers took individual responsibility for their work as teachers. One of them was a supervision teacher, and he had 'iron-control' of what happened in the school and Hedvig says that when he left, discipline standards fell. Another was in charge of the Christmas show and it was great until it was turned into a group effort. And in the classrooms there was good order and the male teachers controlled everything that happened, according to Hedvig.

In her stories, Hedvig embraces the male jargon by emphasizing the humour, the community and the informal solidarity between the teachers when keeping discipline in school. She stands out as a female teacher who was included in the male community. But she also emphasises differences between sexes by implying that all female teachers probably did not feel the same. Her stories fit in well with the discourse of the late 90s where sex differences were stressed and male teachers were described as rational and action-oriented. But the caring side of the role model is toned down, and instead humour and community are included in her stories of the male teachers.

Margret, a retired biology teacher, illustrates a completely different standpoint in her stories about the strict men. After a short break in my first interview with her, she asks if she is telling me the kind of stories I am interested in. I have asked open questions about the school's history and that is what she has been talking about so I give her a green light to continue. Then she delivers a seemingly well prepared story about the strict men in the year 1985. She is the main character in the story and she has named it 'The bullied teacher'.

> **Margret**: I had a few very outspoken and funny and great colleagues. But sometimes they went too far, and they did it verbally. [Håkan: Ok.] So, in the staff common room, when something had happened, they would call these students names. I almost don't dare to say them. 'Bloody piss chicks', occurred. 'Goats', was another, and there were more. I always reacted negatively, my brain said no. I thought it was a bit unpleasant. [Håkan: Yes.] Yes, and I thought that it is in this inner circle and nothing evil would come out of it [Håkan: No.] and so on… But after hearing it a few times. I thought. 'Margret, what would you think if, now I don't have a daughter, but if your daughter went to a school where some of the teachers called her a "Bloody piss chick"? I would think it was horrible'. And then I thought like this, 'If they dare to say such things about students, then I, God damn it, dare to say what I think'. So I told them. And I said exactly like this. 'If I have a student, or if you have your own kid in a school, would you like it if someone said like that? I know it is not meant to be vicious but... You are really nice colleagues; you are superb teachers and the students like you. But can't we try to break this jargon?' And this was delicate. This was not a good [Håkan: No.] thing to say. [Håkan: A bit like swearing in church?] Exactly, but I didn't say any more. And then it was, yes. The next day when I came to school to the staff common room some started to say, 'Hush Margret is coming'. Then I was bullied! (Laughs) (2009-04-20)

Margret finishes the story by telling that they stopped to use 'these words' when they talked about students and after a few months the headmaster gave her his support by saying, 'Well done', and calling her brave. So from her point of view, this is a success story of the breaking of the male jargon. A negative and insensitive masculinity is stressed in her view of the jargon and in naming the story 'The bullied teacher'. In her story, Margret stands out as a female teacher who opposes the male jargon, and differences between the sexes are emphasised, and she also offers the male teachers an alternative, more caring position (Mishler, 1999), through her arguments as a mother and her appeal to them to start thinking as fathers. Her story carries marks of the discourse of struggling against women's subordination, but the father metaphor also calls for a more patriarchal kind of caring.

Fredrik's version of the institutional memory of the strict men has a clear character of a 'retold tale' (Linde 2009, p. 72) because he was not present when the events occurred. He is in the middle of his career and started his work at the school many years after these men had left, so what he tells me is what he has heard from others. Consequently, when he tells his stories, he situates them in the past and treats them like anecdotes about male teachers in a historical context (Freeman, 2010, p. 108) other than his own. They tend to be a part of the history of teachers in a more general sense than the stories of Hedvig and Margret. Fredrik's version of the institutional memory of the strict men relates what he thinks it meant to be a male teacher at Lake School in the past, as illustrated in the following:

> **Fredrik**: But it could be a matter of teacher styles as well. Back then there was an emphasis on subject content. They, they didn't care very much about student-related issues, and I guess no one did in the past, as it is now. That is, one has to discuss things, like (students') non-attendance and such. But back then, in the past, it seemed... at least these originals (teachers); they were so...focused on their school subjects so it was... It was the only thing that mattered. 'Those who didn't care? Who gives a damn, let's do it our way.' On days for teacher training and such, I know they told me, so it was. They perhaps stayed until morning coffee, and then if it didn't suite them they went home instead. [Håkan: Ok.] 'I already know about this' or 'this wasn't interesting' [Håkan: No.] 'I'll go home and read my Physics instead' or 'History' or whatever it was. And they were strong enough, so the headmaster didn't care. It was... they ran their own race, I think. [Håkan: Yes, yes.] I wasn't there [Håkan: No.] but I... that's the way I perceived it. And they were still respected because I guess they were fairly skilled in their subjects and got most students to keep up, I think... But I guess it was more common in the past (2009-06-02).

But still, he uses the institutional memory to position himself as a male teacher today. By calling the male teachers in the past 'originals', and ascribing them a heavy interest in their school subjects and arbitrariness, sharply opposing any kind of external control, he creates a space to position himself as another kind of male teacher. When he talks about his own way of being a teacher he describes himself as a coach, emphasising the importance of getting all students to work together as a team. It is important to him, to create a good atmosphere in the classroom and to work on relationships with the students.

Fredrik does not mention the strictness of the male teachers in the past, but he is influenced by their relaxed attitudes and their sense of humour. He says that the teachers used to have a beer and a smoke in Friday afternoons in the staff room. And he talks about practical jokes they orchestrated. Once a teacher had to show a film to his students and the male colleges changed the videotape to something embarrassing for the teacher. Fredrik says that he and a college tried to link with this tradition, but in a more 'normal level'—for example they circulated some absurd old and boring papers among colleges with an appeal to prepare for a discussion.

By telling his version of the institutional memory, Fredrik takes a stand against some of the messages from the past. For example, in contrast to the strict men, he does not want to overindulge the matter of subject contents or their authoritarian individualistic style. Instead he stands out as a teacher acting as a coach, emphasizing good relations in the classroom and an ability to gain insight into the students' daily life as key elements when he talks of himself. But when it comes to the humorous side of the institutional memory, he is willing to adopt the tradition of practical jokes and maybe a relaxed attitude.

Fredrik does not emphasise differences between the sexes, but rather differences between the past and the present. He takes a stand against an authoritarian way of being a teacher, but his metaphor of a team leader is not so far from the idea of a caring father, and he is amused at a moderate version of the male jargon. Still he opposes the stereotypical image of men when he talks about his social skills and sense of empathy. He is using resources from all the three discourses described above when performing his identity as a male teacher.

CONCLUDING DISCUSSION

The school politics of the Swedish government is based on the idea that men and women have different, culturally defined, and complementary characteristics, which are described as assets. These characteristics are taken for granted and are seldom articulated but they are linked to a discourse where men are seen as rational and action oriented. The male role model is constructed as a caring and authoritarian head of the household and, as I would argue, it has similarities with a traditional gender role. In the political rhetoric, this role model is linked to expectations of more discipline in school and improved results.

When analysing teachers' stories about male teachers in school today and in the past, it becomes clear that constructions of gender is a complex issue. Masculinities are differently constructed in different times and contexts (Connell, 1995). What qualities male teachers might add to school depend on how masculinity is constructed in different contexts and who is telling the story. Not until the notion of 'male role models' is given different meanings in relation to different stories does it become useful. Since Swedish teachers are expected to 'counteract traditional gender roles', it would seem wise to collect many stories, from professionals in school, as a basis for a discussion about gender roles and male role models, instead of using just one rather unarticulated narrative.

These situated stories make the discussion of the use of male role models as an incitement to change in school more complex in terms of changing gender roles as well as improving results in school. Different discourses and different narratives are used when teachers, and others, talk about men in school and there is no such thing as one distinct role model but several, depending on who is telling the story. My analysis of the institutional memory of the strict men in Lake School shows how the teachers tell their stories from their own point of view, highlighting their own gendered professional identities. Similarly, the role model concept is given different meanings, based on gendered values, depending on the point of view of the teller. Thus, more stories (also the inconvenient ones) about the qualities men are supposed to bring to school need to be told, before the male role model concept can be used, as a way to change school. Because teachers are at the centre of gendered constructions in school, their stories and constructions of male teachers in school are vital. Also educational researchers and politicians need to spell out their stories about the qualities men are expected to add to school before spending resources on attracting more men to school.

If the role model concept is used without being linked to different discourses, contexts and situated stories, there is a risk that it will result in a stereotypical view of men in school, thus (re-)producing traditional gender roles rather than counteracting them.

NOTES

[1] Expression first coined in the film *The Rains of Ranchipur* (1955).
[2] According to these international surveys Swedish students' achievement in Mathematics and Science had deteriorated in comparison with previous results.
[3] All names that occur in this text are changed to safeguard the teachers' integrity.
[4] 'The Million Program' was part of an expansive phase of the Swedish welfare policy where the Social Democratic Party took initiative to the building of one million new homes between the years 1965–74.

REFERENCES

Apple, M. W. (2006). Producing inequalities: Neo-liberalism, neo-conservatism, and the politics of educational reform. In H. Lauder, Phillip Brown, Jo-Anne Dillabough & Albert H. Halsey (Eds.), *Education, globalization & social change*, 468–489. New York, NY: Oxford University Press.
Arnesen, A. L., Lahelma, E., & Öhrn, E., (2008). Travelling discourses on gender and education: The case of boys' underachievement. *Nordisk Pedagogik 28*(1), 1–14.
Ball, S. J. (2007). *Education Plc: Understanding private sector participation in public sector education.* Oxton: Routledge.
Björklund, J. (2008a). Många mätningar visar att skolresultaten sjunker [Electronic verion] 27/8 *Svenska Dagbladet.*
Björklund, J. (2008b). Flumskolans företrädare förlorar inflytande [Electronic version] 1/9 *Svenska Dagbladet.*
Björklund, J., & Sabuni, M. (2008). 110 miljoner till jämställdhet i skolan [Electronic version] 11/6 *Dagens Nyheter.*
Connell, R. W. (1995). *Masculinities.* Berkeley: University of California Press.

Freeman, M. (2010). *Hindsight: The promise and peril of looking backward*. New York: Oxford University Press Inc.

Goodson, I. F., & Sikes, P. (2001). *Life history research in educational settings: Learning from lives*. Buckingham: Open University Press.

Goodson, I., & Choi P. L. (2008). Life history and collective memory as methodological strategies: Studying teacher professionalism. *Teacher Education Quarterly, 35*(2), 5–28.

Green, A. (2006). Education, globalization, and the nation state. In H. Lauder, P. Brown, J. A. Dillabough & A. H. Halsey (Eds.) *Education, globalization & social change*, 192–197. New York: Oxford University Press Inc.

Högskoleverket (2009). *Man ska bli lärare: Den ojämna könsfördelningen inom lärarutbildningen* [Rapport 2009:7 R]. Stockholm: Högskoleverket.

Linde, C. (2009). *Working the past: Narrative and institutional memory*. New York: Oxford University Press.

Mishler, E. G. (1999). *Storylines: Craftartists' narratives of identity*. Harvard: Harvard University Press.

Nordberg, M. (2005). *The spearhead of gender equality: Male workers, gender equality, masculinity, femininity and hetronormativity* [Doctorial thesis]. Göteborg: Arkipelag.

Pérez Prieto, H. (2006). *Historien om räven och andra berättelser: Om klasskamrater och skolan på en liten ort—ur ett skol-och livsberättelseperspektiv*. Karlstad: Karlstad University.

Plummer, K. (2006). *Documents of life 2: An invitation to critical humanism*. London: SAGE Publications Ltd.

Skolverket. (2011). Personal i grundskolan 2010/11. http://www.skolverket.se/sb/d/1639 [date 2011-04-21]

SCB. (1985). *Utbildningsstatistisk årsbok 1986*. Stockholm: Statistiska Centralbyrån.

Willis, P. E. (1977). *Learning to labor: How working class kids get working class jobs*. Farnborough: Saxon House.

AFFILIATION

Håkan Löfgren
Institute of Higher Education,
Karlstad University

MARIA DO CARMO MARTINS

8. NARRATIVES AND TESTIMONIES

Hearing the Voices, Writing the Impressions, Changing the Meaning

This chapter arises from the challenge of articulating my research into curriculum and history—specifically curriculum history in relation to my teaching experience in the Brazilian university context. In my work I reflect upon life stories and experiences of schooling, memory and teacher identity construction, memories of schooling and representations (Martins: 2004, 2005, 2007a). I also reflect upon the construction of life stories and memories of schooling through narrative curriculum (Martins, 2007b) and also, as Goodson calls it, 'life politics' (Goodson, 1995, 2005a, 2009).

The potential of life stories in educational research has been a preoccupation of Ivor Goodson and I share with him the belief in the political strength of narratives. Looking at his work I will try to present an original consideration of the Brazilian academic culture, as well as the political and social contexts in which it is produced.

Goodson's sensitivity for matters of power, structures of change, disadvantaged social groups (those without access to power) and his ability to deal with different theories is particularly important for a country like Brazil, which is shaped by a history of colonialism, authoritarianism and a very late blossoming of social and cultural inclusion. In *Personal History and Curriculum Study* (Goodson, 2009) Goodson seeks alternative solutions to educational problems, especially in curriculum. His ideas on teacher's professionalisation take into account the personal, political and social dimensions, articulating the individual life story within the context (life story and life history). Indeed his careful approach to the subject (especially ethical issues) relates greatly to my work in training courses for teachers in Brazil.

An equally important issue for historical studies and narratives, is the emergence of distinct contexts and how to put them into perspective. Thus, I have been working on the potential of life stories, focusing on school memories linking research and teaching, theory and practice (Goodson 2005b).

The chapter that follows is divided in three sections. Firstly, I briefly introduce the context of teacher education in Brazilian universities, the ongoing 'pedagogical battle' and the attempts to develop an undergraduate model for educational policies.

The second section presents the development of the undergraduate discipline 'School and Culture' as an alternative to the rhetoric and consensual historical discourse, which inexorably links curriculum to the institution where it develops. 'Curriculum subjects' in teacher's training was established during the

Ivor F. Goodson, Avril M. Loveless and David Stephens (Eds.), Explorations in Narrative Research, 83–90.

reorganization of degree programs at the university where I work. With the reorganization of degree programs (2002–2005) I recognised a number of conflicts and idiosyncrasies, but I also saw the potential to challenge the predominant model—introduce narratives and change the teacher training model. The third section is concerned with basic aspects of teacher education in Brazil, discussing the 'predominant curriculum model' and highlighting the intrinsic relation between this curricular model and the creation of institutions where this model historically occurred.

THE CONTEXT OF TEACHER EDUCATION: CULTURE AND POLITICS, THE BATTLE FOR PEDAGOGY

Overall, teacher education in Brazilian universities takes place on courses called *'Licenciaturas'*, mostly a set of undergraduate subjects, and it focuses on educational themes such as: mathematics, physics or history, for example—aiming to train teachers to work in the national educational system (public or private). To qualify as teachers they must attend the *'Licenciatura'*. For example, a maths student studies the mathematics curriculum within a classic bachelor's degree, some educational subjects are studied also and it is followed by a probational teaching period.

As for the educational professionals who intend to work in the 'initial grades', or primary education as it was previously known as, they study 'Pedagogy' which includes subjects such as: philosophy, the history of education, the sociology of education, psychology, didactics, curriculum, educational policy and teaching practice, moving on to subjects such as science, Portuguese—with a focus upon literacy (reading and writing) and numeracy.

In both courses the graduates are 'licensed to teach', in other words, they are able to work in a range of positions in public and private teaching institutions; they are also able to apply for positions in public teaching and be members of the so called 'educational professional' group. What differentiates them as teachers is the basic teaching content (the subject) and the age group they teach. Those holding a degree in pedagogy are also able to become educational managers, school principals or pedagogical coordinators.

Although this model has prevailed up to now, its historical development was gradual and complied with the setting up of distinct awarding institutions—Normal Schools,[1] Institutes of Education or Faculties of Education at universities. Tanuri (2000) argued that this process was not only slow but had problems—was ineffectively implemented and demonstrated the need to train more teachers for primary schools, complementary schools and secondary schools.

Also according to Tanuri (2000), the creation of the pedagogy course at the Universidade do Brazil in 1939 was an important milestone in the consolidation of the model of teacher education in the country. This course set up the curricular structure known as '3 + 1'—i.e., three years studying educational subjects, such as: sociology, the psychology of education, plus one year of 'didactics'. In the case of

Pedagogy, the three years of technical content trained educational specialists and the '+1' didactics year trained them to be teachers.

When analysing the policies of teacher education, the pedagogy course can be seen as the course which produces 'educational experts'. It has a politically distinct and central place in academic institutions, as well as in educational policies. It was established as an undergraduate course and was not well regarded by the classical sciences.

Despite criticisms, the '3 + 1' structure of teacher education prevailed in the years following and it received additional support in the educational reforms of the 60s and 70s during the period of dictatorship in Brazil. It was characterised by extensive political interventionism in higher education and in the basic structure of the educational system.

During this period there were two major educational reforms in Brazil—both were anti-democratic in character, and to a greater extent 'prescribed'. Because they were seen as closely tied into the authoritarian ruling forces, schools and universities they were generally discredited. This was a period of repression of the student's movement and a gradual suppression of alternative proposals, such as the vocational, experimental or libertarian pedagogies.

Regarding the training of teachers, the university reform of 1968 saw pedagogy and didactics as 'skills' to be acquired by candidates for teaching—a technical complementary education to the bachelor's degree. Often, in a system where private colleges proliferated they had nothing in common with the forms of knowledge production found in the biggest Brazilian universities.

This precarious situation continued even when the military dictatorship ended. It remained thus, right up to 2000 when teacher education and especially the curriculum became the focus of educational reforms. The '3 + 1' model, however, continued.

This two part model qualified those wanting to work with children (at nurseries and primary schools) and those who wanted to work with school subjects. In 2002 and 2006 the National Curricular Guidelines were published in Brazil; the first guidelines targeted the training of basic education teachers and the later one— Pedagogy.[2] Although both were *Licenciaturas* and focused upon teaching as the basis of the teacher training, they had different views of what was a teacher and what their training should be like.

As I have shown, part of this curriculum was a training period which could be pursued in parallel with or, after achieving bachelor degree level. It was usual and fairly common in the 70s, 80s and also 90s that a physicist, a mathematician or a linguist, in times when the job market was in bad shape, could go back to university or to a private college and attend the '*Licenciatura*'. Thus, with only a handful of subjects, and in a very short time, the student would be entitled to work as a teacher

Another problem with the predominant model of teacher's training in Brazil was the creation of an image of 'Ideal Teacher'—teachers as professionals, with new skills in a kind of non-personal or non-subjective training (Freitas, 1992). During their under graduate courses, they acquired abilities and didactic techniques.

The reforming of the '*Licenciaturas*' at UNICAMP happened in a context of intense dispute. This curriculum battle, saw the subject of 'School and Culture' emerge as a cultural alternative. The subject became official in the 2005 UNICAMP curriculum.

The perception of some professors of the reforms was that they enabled them to create 'School and Culture', as an alternative to conservative curriculum, and an innovative curricular space which was previously occupied by didactics and teaching practices specific to each degree, be it history, maths, geography... challenging a classical teacher graduation model.

NARRATIVES & 'THE SCHOOL AND CULTURE' SUBJECT

'School and Culture' was a curricular component that was defined as 'an open discipline' in a recent seminar at Campinas (see Prof Oliveira Jr. 2008).[3] It was offered by a group of distinguished professors at the Faculty of Education to students from varying study fields (the natural sciences, humanities and arts, mostly at the start of their undergraduate course).

The students were and are, those who had recently gone through elementary school and still possessed many of the pedagogic schooling habits considered necessary for their study of school curriculum. It is important also to note that the competition for university places is very high. These students expect an education at university that is school related and also completely innovative. But the reality of their university education causes them to be sometimes confused about what they really want from teacher training.

Paradoxically, as they enter the undergraduate course and face a route that leads to teacher training they can be seen to be rather critical of their school's former teachers (with few exceptions) and alienated from Brazilian educational policies.

These student 'narratives' are the focus of many aspects of my work. I have been working with these students in order to promote and explore these different narrative stories. As previously stated (Martins, 2007), the narratives are made up of memories and personal thoughts, articulated in different languages and they bring forth, as a cultural artefact, memory, personal expression from the cultural milieu in which they are created.

Memory is key to their narratives and images of school memory emerge as important themes for identifying the subject, the lived processes and the possibility of keeping alive their desires and fears. Memory links reason to emotion; it refers to the senses and the ability to deal with many temporalities and spaces. With it, we activate thinking, updating the past in the present.

Working collectively, we produced together a school setting and a historical context in which the students were involved, supported in discussions by ideas of memory (see Sarlo, 2007). However, in order to further understand the school as a cultural production, we also produced narratives using audiovisual resources (photographing the school space and creating short films).

We also worked with two distinct types of narratives—films and literature—analytically constructing and deconstructing images and representations in a selective discussion. This gave rise to the concept of the school as a metaphor for the 'black-box'.[4]

The issue of narrative has been important in this undergraduate learning context, for enabling an articulation of the aesthetic, historical and the political. They allow a repositioning of opinions and in 'the war of speeches' they relativised the reigning political powers.

CHANGING DIRECTION: QUESTIONING THE TRADITIONAL MODEL OF TEACHER'S TRAINING

When the students analysed the narratives they were able to question the pedagogic element of their academic education. Tanuri (2000) argues that the history of teacher training in Brazil has walked hand in hand with discussions of a 'specialised curriculum' and, above all, its content.

There are plenty of studies about the history of 'Normal Schools' in Brazil (see Araújo, Freitas, Lopes, 2008) and also studies into the creation, implementation and functioning of the Institutes of Education in the 1930s (Evangelista, 1997; Vidal, 2001; Martins, 1996), as well as the creation of the 'Faculty of Philosophy, Sciences and Languages' which initiated this training for high school teachers in didactics (Mendonça, 1994; Bontempi Jr, 2007). Most of these studies also show the social construction of teacher and the teaching profession, the latter being strongly marked by moral, political and economic disputes.

Bontempi Jr (2007), for instance, shows that the effective model of teacher training had already been established in the Faculty of Philosophy, Science and Languages of the University of São Paulo in 1938 and highlights that the creation of didactics within that Faculty was beset by numerous conflicts between university professors and education teachers. According to Bontempi Jr, this discreditation of didactics found some support among many university professors.

Since then training has taken place which follows a basic content: 'Structure and Functioning of Education', 'Psychology of Learning', 'Psychology of Adolescence', 'Methodology/Didactics of Teaching' (history, mathematics or arts, for instance), 'Teaching Practice' (history, mathematics or arts) and 'Supervised Internship'.

Coincidently with the great expansion of higher education in twentieth century Brazil there was also the 'Licenciaturas'. It was up to the school teacher to find through didactics the path to transform scientific knowledge into something teachable.

One of the strongest and most forceful criticisms of this model was exactly the lack of articulation amongst the disciplines, or even an overview of the educational system and subject of learning. In general terms, the subject 'Structure and Functioning of Education' was restricted to an understanding of educational legislation and the principles of curricular prescription. In psychology, which amounted to almost two thirds of the subjects that 'prepared' the students for didactics and practices, the subjects of education and cognitive processes were studied separately. Part of the criticism arose over the separation between the content of bachelor's degrees and the 'Licenciaturas'.

M. D. C. MARTINS

In the case of teacher training it is obvious that the reforms tended to carry very clearly three levels of conflicts: on the personal belief level, the institutional and the macro-political level. Looking at the issues surrounding 'School and Culture', we can clearly see that Brazil has an academic and cultural context in which prescription is as an expression of power groups in historic conflict; the 'ideal teacher' emerges as an object of political dispute and higher education still produces more social differentiation than equity. But the work on narratives however has allowed us some questioning and understanding of these educational models and historical conflicts.

NOTES

[1] The 'Normal School' was the institution that maintained the 'Normal Course', a course for teacher's training at secondary level. The first Normal School was built in 1835, in Niteroi, R.J. These schools educated teachers to work in the primary school.
[2] Resolution CNE/CP, 02/18/2002 and Resolution CNE/CP 05/18/2006.
[3] Working documents produced by the seminar. This was subsequently taken over by the 'Departamento de Educação, Conhecimento, Linguagem e Arte' (DELART), and informed Public Policies for the Formation of Teachers in the Faculty of Education at UNICAMP.
[4] The school as a 'black box' is a metaphor used by Dominique Juliá, in the article 'A cultura escolar como objeto histórico'. *Revista Brasileira de História da Educação*, n. 1, 2001.

REFERENCES

Araujo, J. C. S., Freitas, A. G. B., & Lopes, A. P. C. (2008). *As escolas normais no Brasil, do império à república*. Campinas: Editora Átomo e Alínea.
Bontempi Júnior, B. (2007). A incorporação do Instituto de Educação pela FFCL-USP: Hipóteses para entender um campo cindido. *Reunião Anual da Anped*, 30a.
Carvalho, A. M. P. (1992). Reformas nas licenciaturas: A necessidade de uma mudança de paradigma mais do que mudança curricular. *Em Aberto*, Brasília, ano *12*, 54.
Di Pietro S., & Pineau, P. (2008). *Aseo y presentación: Un ensayo sobre la estética escolar*. Buenos Aires: El Autor.
Evangelista, O. (1998). A formação do professor em nível universitário—O Instituto de Educação da Universidade de São Paulo (1934–1938). SP: PUC—Tese de Doutoramento.
Freitas, L. C. (1992). Em direção a uma política para formação de professores. *Em Aberto*, Brasília, ano *12*, 54.
Goodson, I. F. (1995). Dar voz ao professor: As histórias de vida dos professores e o seu desenvolvimento profissional. In Nóvoa, A (org.) *Vida de Professores*, Portugal: Porto Editora.
Goodson, I. F. (1997). *A construção social do currículo*. Lisboa: Educa.
Goodson, I. F. (2005a). Sponsoring the teacher's voice. In I. Goodson *Learning, Curriculum and Life Politics: The selected works of Ivor Goodson*. New York: Routledge, Taylor & Francis.
Goodson, I. F. (2005b). Representing Teachers: Bringing teachers back in. In I. Goodson, *Learning, Curriculum and Life Politics: The selected works of Ivor Goodson*. New York: Routledge, Taylor & Francis.
Goodson, I. F. (2009). Personal history and curriculum study. In E. Short & L. Waks *Leaders in curriculum studies: Intellectual self-portrait*, Rotterdam Boston and Taipei: Sense.
Martins, M. C. (2004). E se o outro é o professor? Reflexões acerca de currículo e história de vida. In S. Gallo, R. M. de Souza (Eds.) *Educação do Preconceito: Ensaios sobre poder e resistência*, 103–118. Alinea, Campinas.

Martins, M. C. (2005). Eu me lembro de escolhi... In A. Corbalan (Ed.) *Enredados por la educación, la cultura e la política*. Biblos.

Martins, M. C. (2007a). Historia, currículo y prácticas pedagógicas: sobre memorias y narrativas. In M. C. Herrera (Ed.) *Encrucijadas e indicios sobre America Latina: Educación, cultura y política*. Bogotá: Universidad Pedagógica Nacional.

Martins, M. C. (2007b). Histórias do currículo e currículos narrativos: Possibilidades de investigação na história social do conhecimento. *Revista Pro-Posições*, FE/UNICAMP, 18.

Martins, A. M. S.(1996). *Dos anos dourados aos anos de zinco: Análise histórico-cultural da formação do educador no Instituto de Educação do Rio de Janeiro*. FE/UFRJ. (Tese de Doutorado).

Mendonça, A. W. P. C. (1994). Universidade e formação de professores: Uma perspectiva histórica. *Cadernos de Pesquisa*, São Paulo, *90*, 36–44. Carlos Chagas/Cortez.

Oliveira, Jr. (2008). *As ações do Delart na proposição e realização das Políticas Públicas de Formação de Professores na FE/Unicamp* (Documento de Trabalho cedido pelo autor).

Sarlo, B. (2007). *Tempo Passado: Cultura da memória e a guinada subjetiva*. MG: Editora UFMG e Companhia das Letras.

Tanuri, L. M. (2000). História da Formação de Professores. In D. Saviani, L.A Cunha, M. M. C. Carvalho (orgs) 500 Anos de educação escolar. *Revista Brasileira de Educação*, *14*, 61–88.

Vidal, D. G. (2001). *O exercício disciplinado do olhar: Livros, leituras e práticas de formação docente no Instituto de Educação do Distrito Federal (1932-1937)*. Bragança Paulista. USF (Coleção Estudos CDAPH).

AFFILIATION

Maria do Carmo Martins
Departamento de Educação, Conhecimento, Linguagem e Arte
Universidade Estadual de Campinas

CIARAN SUGRUE

9. THE PERSONAL IN THE PROFESSIONAL LIVES OF SCHOOL LEADERS

Relating Stories within Stories

INTRODUCTION

One of the most persistent recurring phrases espoused by those who enter the teaching profession is 'making a difference' (Christopher Day and Gu, 2010; Chris. Day, Sammons, Stobart, Kingston, and Gu, 2007) in the lives of learners, and this individual personal-professional commitment is challenged and in some instances undermined by persistent policy impulses to control by means of various technologies of accountability (Ball, 2008; Ciaran Sugrue and Dyrdal Solbrekke, 2011). Consequently, there is 'increased pressures upon teachers in all phases of education, not only to 'produce better results', but also to be more directly accountable for the success or failure of their pupils' (Day and Gu, 2010, p. 21). As the twin towers of autonomy and accountability have come to dominate the educational reform landscape, teacher and principal 'resilience' (Day et al., 2007) as well as 'vulnerability' (Geert Kelchtermans, 2011; G. Kelchtermans, Piot, and Ballet, 2011), have come to the fore as part of a survival repertoire in such turbulent times. Resilience is defined as: 'the capacity to 'bounce back' to recover strength or spirit quickly and efficiently in the face of adversity, is closely allied to a strong sense of vocation, self-efficacy and motivation... (Day et al., 2007, p. 195). Similarly, in Kelchtermans's work, the sense of vulnerability is heightened by contemporary conditions of teachers (and principals') work; a condition he describes as:

> ... always... feeling that one's professional identity and moral integrity, as part of being 'a proper teacher', are questioned and that valued workplace conditions are thereby threatened or lost. (Kelchtermans, 2011, pp. 118–119)

School leaders in this contemporary educational landscape are all too aware of the tensions and contradictions between their agentic responsibilities to be task oriented, while from an existential perspective feeling insecure and vulnerable. Such conditions are pressuring more focused attention on the interface between the personal and the professional realm(s), to figure the various means through and by which individual actors access and use as a significant resource the life story as a means of lending ballast to professional disposition and action—to constructing a personal/professional (narrative) identity.

This chapter is in four parts. First, a theoretical lens is constructed that both situates subsequent data analysis as well as provides tools for thinking about the relationship between the personal and professional spheres in contemporary life and work. Second, a brief background to the data set, its creation and analysis are indicated. Third, after a brief biographical introduction to Fred (the participant) analysis of evidence is re-presented in two distinct phases—formative influences, followed by professional identity formation and the intertwining of the personal in the process. Fourth, the concluding section reflects on life history narrative as a means of understanding professional life and work and how professional learning policy and practice might be more appropriately tailored to such concerns.

THEORETICAL PERSPECTIVES

The warning that 'life history can seriously damage your understanding' is well made (I. F. Goodson, 2008, p. 89). Yet, it is indispensable to the task on hand. I subscribe to the view that: '... personal narrative and the life story have arrived' (McAdams, 2008). As 'trait theory' and issues of character are being left behind in favour of more 'evidence-based' practice (Denzin, 2009; Hargreaves, 1996), a more myopic and bounded agenda is being privileged and this limits both educational possibilities for learners and is reductionist in its implications for the renewal of professional practice. Against this narrowing of horizons and thus also limiting possible futures, it is necessary to distinguish between life story and the construction of life histories. While not in opposition to a life story per se, its avowed intent is to 'create a different story to that of the personal life story' (Goodson, 2008, p. 90); it is necessary to understand its provenance as 'a story of action within a theory of context' (I. F. Goodson, 1991, p. 173). Such concerns render it both possible and appropriate to concur that the 'subject-matter of stories is human action. Stories are concerned with human attempts to progress to a solution, clarification or unravelling of an incomplete situation' (Polkinghorne, 1995, p. 7). It is the very incompleteness, uncertainty and unpredictability of situatedness that attaches significance to the agency of actors, yet there are elements of personal and professional scripts that remain open to continuing authorship. Such authoring is autobiographical, the positioning of 'selves in relation to general or prevailing values' (Erben, 1998, p. 1), on the one hand, and the wider shifting sociological landscape on the other, an act of imagination (Taylor, 2004/ 2007 4th edition; Wright Mills, 1959).

However attractive such renderings of reality may be in a 'runaway' (Giddens, 2002) or 'liquid' (Bauman, 2000/2006) world, this narrating of reality poses particular challenges to the researcher: '... the issue of how far the informant's words are left to speak for themselves and how much commentary and analysis there should be' (I. F. Goodson, and Sikes, P., 2001, p. 37). Such considerations take on heightened significance in the current context since the narration of stories and the particular identities crafted by my school leader informants (see below) is not my primary consideration. Rather, it is what may be gleaned by moving back and forth between the personal and the professional, in so far as these are distinguishable and separate entities. By occupying this liminal space within the narrated stories and espoused identities of my informants, there is a sense in which I am exploiting their renderings, occupying them for a particular purpose, to seek insight into the 'back story'—the life, and how this becomes a source and re-source in the ongoing construction of one's narrative. While my informants were all principals, the primary focus here is the life and work rather than roles and responsibilities.

Aspects of recent life history work is potentially generative and offers an addition to the theoretical considerations already articulated—another element of an interpretive lens through which to undertake analysis (Archer, 2000, 2003, 2007). Archer offers a spectrum of possibilities for understanding the 'internal conversation', modes of being in, and engaging with, the world that are deeply rooted in biography, while not being discrete, thus they interact and overlap, while individuals have a tendency to be more at home, either as—a communicative, autonomous or meta-reflexive. Although Archer readily acknowledges that we are all communicative reflexives, those who are most comfortable with this modus vivendi tend to deal with their concerns 'by talking them through with other people'(Archer, 2007, p. 101) By tending to be more cautious and conservative, more open to influence of immediate community, its prevailing norms and values. For the more autonomous reflexive, they typically seek challenge and are engaged by tasks, pitting their skills and expertise against challenge while attracted to 'novelty, variety and flexibility' (2007, p. 291), building expertise while relishing yet another 'project'; 'they are willingly lending themselves to *elastication*' (p. 293). By contrast, meta-reflexives tend to devote more time to the internal conversation in a more sustained self-questioning manner, sometimes leading to isolated rumination, and the accolade 'loner', sometimes to the point of inaction through self-doubting introspection. Consequently:

... pronounced meta-reflexives have greater difficulties in defining a satisfying and sustainable modus vivendi for themselves than do markedly communicative or autonomous reflexives. They share neither the localised normativity of the former nor the self-confident individualism of the latter. (Archer, 2007, p. 95)

It may be suggested, without foreclosing on understandings of leaders' identities that in the current policy climate of increasingly 'scripted' leadership under the twin towers of autonomy and accountability, the pervasive influences of neo-liberal ideologically inspired new public management reform agenda, that the place and space for meta-reflexives in school leadership positions may not feature too prominently in recruitment and retention considerations (MacBeath, et al., 2009). These perspectives provide further fruit for thought as attention is turned to data and its analysis across the porous boundaries of personal 'back stories' and professional identities.

DATA SET AND ANALYSIS

Approximately 60 life history interviews, conducted with sixteen Irish primary school principals in the past decade (2000–2008) comprise the extensive data set that is drawn on in this chapter. Some of this evidence has been utilised in previous publications (C. Sugrue, 2005; C. Sugrue, and Furlong, C., 2002), while other work is in process. Each participant was interviewed at least twice for more than an hour on each occasion; all interviews were transcribed, and open coding ensued using NVivo. For the purposes of this chapter, however, I focus on the life history of one individual, while in the construction and analysis of his story, remain mindful of the wider context of its situatedness, as well as the changing educational and socio-cultural landscape of Ireland over the past four decades, widely documented elsewhere while an important hinterland in the interpretation of evidence and the construction of the story in context (Arnold, 2009; Cleary, 2007; Cooney, 1986; Cooper, 2009; Corcoran, 2002; O' Connell, 2001; F. O' Toole, 2009; Fintan O' Toole, 2010).

Fred: A Biographical Sketch

Fred received his formal education in rural Ireland. He completed a two-year programme of initial teacher education in 1969, and commenced his teaching career in the same year in a large urban all-boys primary school in Dublin. He came from a farming family in the Midlands. Within the next two years, after some persuasion, he was appointed principal of a two-teacher primary school close to his native heath. By the time he availed of early retirement in 2010, he had been principal for four decades, while in more recent years he presided over a major school building project and school expansion, thus in the latter part of his career his status altered to that of administrative principal in a school with eight teachers. Throughout he dabbled in farming, a biographical inheritance, while he also invested in his own learning—completing a primary degree, postgraduate study in Development Education, while in-between he relocated his entire family to take up the challenge of teaching in Sub-Saharan Africa (SSA). On retirement, he has returned to a remote area of this vast and intriguing landscape to work with teachers and school principals. His wife enjoyed her own career in teaching, and they have three adult children, while one child died shortly after birth. This is merely the bare bones of Fred's biography, enough to give the reader a sense of the character in the remainder of this unfolding drama; an exploration of the 'sound track' of his biography and how it has been harnessed in the ongoing choreography of his leadership/professional identity.

Fred: Disentangling the Life and the Work

As the first phase in this life history, aspects of early socialisation, family circumstances and formal education, shape the persona of Fred in the making— they lay down important elements of the backing track to his life and work. This section is in two parts, beginning with formative influences, and followed by the professional track that is overlaid on what I am regarding as the original soundtrack, though the former is continually open to being influenced and re-scored by the other, and visa versa. Due to space limitations both elements are illustrated only.

Family, Formal Schooling: Formative Influences

While acknowledging the porous nature of biography and identity, it is reasonable to suggest that some (early) experiences are particularly formative, thus leaving indelible residues on the character and persona of the bearer. Fred initially identifies himself as 'the middle child in a family of five children', the son of a small dairy farmer, while he also identifies his country of origin, signalling the significance of place in Irish identity more generally. Fred traversed a county boundary to attend a town school, while leaving himself open permanently to being 'slagged' regarding inter-county rivalry in Gaelic Football. He describes much of his primary school experience as 'a succession of pretty awful teachers' while he immediately switches to a language resonant with Biblical overtones when he states:

> ...and then when I was in fourth class I was kind of saved. A man from Mayo, [names teacher], God be good to him! An absolutely lovely man, a gentleman, he was my teacher for fourth, fifth and sixth class. And I'm basically a teacher... (Int. 1, 2000)

He reveals subsequently that it was what this teacher was able to do for children that inspired him, while he also provides important insights into perceptions and prejudices between town and country. Corporal punishment was pervasive in schools and wider society, and the young Fred's sense that his fellow pupil should have been 'manly' enough to take his punishment resonates with wider version of masculinity as well as indicates the lack of respect for children and their place in society. He states:

> [names town where he attended primary school] was a rough town. It still has a very rough tail to it, but it was a rough town. There were some real rough guys, and almost out of control guys in the class. Yeah there were. And I remember a teacher emm... going to slap a guy and this was back in the '50s like. And yer man pulled his hand and he held out the other hand for the teacher, and he had a glove on it. And then when the teacher took off the glove, yer man held out this hand and he had a glove back on this hand. I remember being absolutely appalled by; he wouldn't just take what was coming... (Int. 1, 2000)

Challenging authority had been witnessed, while manliness was marked (no pun intended!) by enduring punishment. By contrast, Fred's 'mentor' was inspiring: 'He brought the best out in children', he engaged the pupils through drama, and while he did 'slap kids now and again' his more lasting impression on Fred was that 'what he had was a great 'grá' [love]for teaching,' most likely to be construed in more contemporary language as 'passion' (Christopher Day and Gu, 2010; Chris. Day, et al., 2007).

There were no secondary schools available locally; he attended a Diocesan seminary regionally as a boarder, beginning in the early 1960s at a time in Ireland when universal access to secondary schooling had yet to be introduced, in 1967. He describes his transition from secondary school to college thus:

... at seventeen then I did my leaving cert. and applied for training, wanted to be a primary school teacher basically because of this man's influence. And eh came up here[1] and did an interview and I thought I made and absolute bags of it. And eh was delighted when I got the call, spent two years here in Pats, '67–69. Eh. had a ball of a time. Didn't drink but really enjoyed the experience here, having come out of boarding school in the sense I found Pat's very, a great free place, great place to make friends, develop yourself, have fun (Int. 1, 2000).

Getting 'the call', apart from its vocational overtones, was highly prized in rural Ireland for several decades of the twentieth century. It was a passport to status, security and a state pension when for a significant proportion of each cohort of school leavers, emigration was the reality.

During this time, and prior to the introduction of a Bachelor of Education degree as the entry requirement for primary teachers (introduced in 1974), professional identity formation is strongly if not pervasively influenced by concerns with character and morality, to the possible detriment of developing expertise in terms of understanding education, and building pedagogical knowledge (Karseth, 2011). Emphasis on moral formation is consistent with the 'call'; that there are those who are chosen to be teachers, natural born teachers, thus there is little to be learned— the chosen are already 'saved', a disposition that works against professional learning across the lifespan (Britzman, 1986, 1989, 1991). However, in Fred's family history, resonances of 'the call' run deeper as he reveals later in the same interview, where vocation, and the status of the religious life was highly prized, particularly in rural Ireland. He explains:

I had an uncle, a parish priest, my father's brother. And my mother had two sisters, nuns. And emm... I remember once or twice she'd said to me would you ever consider the church? So even at that stage I couldn't see why you had to be celibate to be... admitting that I was a late developer from the point of view of women and so on... (Int. 1, 2000)

There is a strong sense therefore that the primary call was one to religious life, but its closely associated relative was the secular vocation of teaching which was populated to a significant degree by religious, particularly principalship. Not surprisingly, within this religiously controlled world of teacher formation, a significant element of the formation was to suppress sexuality, thus all males were to be either celibate or late developers! Fred again returns to its influences when he describes his first ventures into the profession having secured his first teaching position with the same mischievous humour and irony evident above. The large single sex boys' school was:

... an absolutely fabulous place to start. And eh... emm... I was quite happy there, and then in '70 I started a degree at night in UCD (University College Dublin), probably just for something to do, to keep me off the streets, keep me away from women. You know, a young lad like that, you wouldn't want to be too exposed to women, at too early an age (Int. 1, 2000).

If celibacy is not pursued then deferred sexual gratification certainly is the desired secular state by the regulating authorities, and keeping 'off the streets' reflects rural prejudice about the dangers and temptations of 'the bright lights'.

Having received the call, Fred indicated that he, 'felt ten foot tall' and this feeling he explains as being due to the perception that 'there was definitely a status involved in getting the call. There was. Emm, it, the perception was you had to be fierce brainy to get the call to train.'

In the following extract, Fred conveys a strong sense of the young urban professional, and while a car was not affordable, acquiring transport provided opportunity and mobility as well as status, yet beneath the surface the celibate homophobic/ heterosexuality of male institutions lurks, continuing its subterranean influences on identity and disposition. He says:

> Well I had graduated to having a motorbike at that stage. And emmm... and I had first arts done and at that stage I was playing rugby at that stage...and at UCD at night. I was having a full life. And then the local school, it would have been the school, the nearest school to me in my own parish ... (Int. 1, 2000)

For many primary teachers, given their intellectual calibre and social background, one of the (many) attractions of securing a teaching position in the capital was the possibility of studying for a degree on a part-time basis.

Professional Call: The Call of 'Home'

Being summoned to come 'home' provides an ironic twist to the 'call' and the combined forces of his mother being pressured by the local parish priest who was also manager of the local two-teacher school, the repeated use of the phrase 'that stage' takes on heightened significance. It was a time in his life he was greatly enjoying and his initial reaction to the summons to come home, not surprisingly was resisted. The manager had been informed by the Department of Education (now the DES) that if he could not secure the services of a qualified teacher, the school would be closed. There had been particular difficulties with the behaviour of the principal, parents had withdrawn their children as a consequence, thus the viability of the school was at stake. After the principal resigned:

> ... the manager, applied three times for a teacher, wasn't successful. No trained teachers answered the ad. The department told him if you don't get a trained teacher, were going to shut the school. He went to me mother, he knew I was in training or a teacher in Dublin, he went to me mother, asked her would I be interested. She asked me and I said no. And then he came back a second time and said well if he doesn't take the job ... we have to close the school. The department have said they'll close the school. Now this was in 1971. So in August '71 I came home... (Int. 1, 2000)

The teacher who had 'saved' him years earlier, was by then principal of another rural school close by and he sought him out for advice and counsel. His strategic thinking was that Fred had nothing to lose and much to gain:

> And he basically put all the options ahead of me. He said sure look, can't you play rugby down here, can't you finish the University from here. Eh and he said and I'll guarantee you one thing, it'll be the best move you'll ever make. You'll never look back. Emm from the point of view of satisfaction, from the point of view of putting your own stamp on something (Int. 1, 2000).

Coming from a farming background, being his own boss and being able to put his own stamp on things had enormous appeal to the young Fred. In this regard also, that strong streak of independence if not rugged individualism characteristic of farmers in general, he reveals is part of the canvas of his personal biography and family history. Compromise, practicality, social reality, as well as deferred gratification are evident when he reveals, regarding his parent's marriage: 'she was from... farming stock. My father and her were a match, match made. And he was 18 years older that her, and my dad was a real farmer, bachelor kind of almost. And he was fifty-three when I was born.' Fred's mother's education had been cut short just after she commenced secondary school, very much a minority pursuit at the time, since her mother got ill and as the eldest (girl) she was obliged to fill the void, and take responsibility. Not unusually, due to its embeddedness in her own biography 'she put great store on learning'. It may be suggested that, precisely because her own education was cut short, she was determined that this would not be the fate of her own offspring. Having actually been a bachelor for most of his life, Fred's father was accustomed to doing things without consultation, perhaps with a streak of stubbornness also. Fred provides insight into his father's modus vivendi while indicating also that he continues to remain in touch with his farming roots:

> ...my father was a dreamer as well as a farmer. He was into Shorthorns when everyone else was into Friesians. And when everyone else was into Herefords and making money, he had Shorthorned bulls, and nobody wanted Shorthorns. He was probably so far ahead of his time, like, you'd get a fortune for Shorthorn bulls now (Int. 1, 2000).

Perhaps then, this complex combination of influences and respect for authority contributed to Fred's decision to leave the bright lights behind and return to his native heath. He recognised he was entering into:

> ... the great unknown but I reckoned... the fact that it was a challenge. And I like challenges, I suppose, that's the sort of guy I am. I'm always looking for some windmill to tilt at. And this was a windmill to tilt at (Int. 1, 2000).

Departing from his urban school colleagues and surroundings for a troubled context was an emotional affair:

> And I remember walking up the long corridor in [names school] with me box of bits and pieces, and I was actually crying. And I, in a way I, when I

walked into [names new school], the school couldn't go anywhere but up...
(Int. 1, 2000)

These life story highlights provide sufficient evidence to suggest tensions in his 'make up' between the autonomous reflexive, who loves a challenge and is not averse to disjuncture, while being influenced by community—familiar and local, an interesting juxta-positioning. Perhaps, the more judicious observation at this juncture, as part of Fred's transition to a leadership position is the observation that:

> The continuous exercise of our reflexive powers, which is what makes us 'active agents'—those who can exercise some governance in and over their own lives—is always a fragile property, ever liable to suspension (Archer, 2007, p. 96).

PERSONAL BACKING TRACK & PROFESSIONAL IDENTITY: UNDERSTANDING THE 'INTERNAL CONVERSATION'

For this section, I have repeatedly trawled Fred's transcripts (four in all), paying particular attention to elements that recur across them—such matters as—mention of his father, his spouse, how he likes a challenge, commitment to community, a sense of vocation that transcends remuneration and 'playing fast and loose' with the rules; these are recurring motifs that appear consistent with Fred's view of himself. While he appears to be most 'at home' as an autonomous reflexive, he displays elements of the communicative and meta dimensions also.

Making a Mark

Having returned 'home', and realising that the school had lost credibility in the eyes of parents, he did not delay in taking on the challenge. He states:

> I was two weeks in the school, I called a meeting of parents. And I had a chairperson, or a manager at the time there as well, because I wasn't confident enough. But eh... I basically set up a parent teacher association...
> (Int. 1, 2000)

At national level parents associations were still in the distant future, Fred needed both support and funds. He is clear about the mixture of motives:

> Now, I suppose I had a mercenary motive there too because I reckoned we needed a lot, I needed a budget. I had lots of plans for schools, and rather than curse the darkness, I wanted to be able to spend money (Int. 1, 2000).

A child-centred, progressive curriculum had been introduced nationally in 1971, thus movement away from a 3Rs curriculum would require resource materials across the curriculum (C. Sugrue, 1997).

In a more visceral sense his evidence points to the independent farmer perhaps more realisable in a small school situation: 'every principal thinks that their own school it the best because they're putting their own stamp on it. But I feel that in education that small is beautiful' (Int. 1, 2000). Being a small and independent school has its attractions and its challenges:

> It's the kids that matter here. And after that I suppose maybe, just the sort of guy I was, I was always looking for challenges. I believed that putting our own stamp on the school, we did things differently, we did them the way I decided (Int. 1, 2000).

This cluster of components is part of his personal soundtrack that features as motif in the on-going identity construction under various guises, and these are illustrated in the remainder of this section.

Relishing a Challenge

An early example of his agency and autonomy are captured in the following vignette:

> I wanted a library, and I got onto the country librarian and badgered him. I remember when he drove out, he had an old battered Ford, no, no, what do you call it, Opel Kadett, with a box, a huge box of books in the boot for me. And he gave me that box of books, and then every so often I'd ring him up and say can we change them. I'd drive over with them and we'd change them. And I didn't give a damn, I didn't ask other schools what are you doing, and I don't believe in doing that in the sense that emm... like I think, if you have to all the time check with somebody else, I think that principal's have a sense of leadership, and have a go at it, try it (Int. 1, 2000).

Fred recognises that his restlessness for a challenge has a downside, even if it staves off the possibility of boredom. He signals: 'I think that's a failing with me, sometimes I don't finish, I'll nine-tenths solve a problem but the actual final tying of the knot, I'll have gone on to something else' (Int. 1, 2000).

Being his Father's Son

Fred has retained his interest in farming, being his father's son—keeping stock, and growing trees. This is both a hobby, therapeutic, and provides additional income also. He paints this particular element of his persona in the following terms:

> Yeh, well you see I don't play golf, I'm not old enough to play golf. You see I suppose I was a farmer's son and I like the environment. And my Dad had a very strong influence on me about trees and that sort of thing; he was that sort of man. And like about the short horn bulls. Like he wasn't going to follow the crowd. If he felt something was instinctively right, he'd do it and I'm kind of the same. And I was always into trees and that's why I planted the Christmas trees just I reckoned how are my kids gonna go through college and sure I'll chance it (Int. 1, 2000).

The more professional side of this persona is commitment to community, not just the immediate community of the school. In this regard, there has been a succession of projects, that befit an autonomous reflexive from fund raising to card playing during winter months, to a significant computer initiative, and in more recent times a major building project. In all of these endeavours Fred has attempted to merge the interests of community with the school to maximise the use of resources and facilities.

One example emerges at the end of the second interview when he states: 'I suppose it comes back to the teacher I had, that teacher made a big difference to me as the kids in the class, I would like to make a difference. I think I am arrogant to say it is a vocation' (Int. 2, 2000).

'Giving Back'—Vocation Renewed?

There is nothing arrogant about Fred's assertion of vocation. Throughout a career, that sense is either reaffirmed or diluted, and in his case, personal tragedy intensifies that commitment, and is shared by his partner. A child of theirs lives only for hours after birth, and in mid-career they are forced by circumstance to re-appraise.

> ... we felt maybe life has been very good to us, maybe it's time to give something back now. And it was kinda that motivation that maybe we'll go on, it sounds fierce pious that we'll give something back but that was our motivation in going... to teach abroad but in actual fact we got far more out of it than we put into it. It was a fabulous experience. Another side of it to is we were half way through our teaching careers almost and to give me personally, the gee up for the last lap, I think something like this was needed (Int. 2, 2000).

Fired by this experience, immediately on his return, Fred completed a Masters in Development Studies, yet another challenge. This vocational turn, this teaching adventure, heightened his sense of vocation, perhaps more in a spiritual rather than a pedagogical sense, and he describes his teaching in subsequent years as connected to world issues regarding social justice, while encouraging a sense of fairness among his pupils through fund raising etc.

This cocktail of idealism and pragmatism also enables Fred to see himself as an autonomous reflexive in both consort and conflict with his more communicative alter ego.

Challenged to Care Too Much?

Fred indicates that in seeking out new challenges, he has repeatedly got a buzz from his professional life, but that this has come at a price: being absent from greater involvement with his children while feeling guilty about leaving the domestic sphere primarily to his spouse: luckily in a sense [names wife] was the homemaker and probably still is the homemaker. When I'm down making hay and pruning trees she's still the homemaker. So that's a regret, that's a regret. On a professional level, I don't think so, I still hope, maybe I have my head in the clouds, maybe I'm not a realist, but I still hope that we're doing a good job, that the parents believe we're doing a good job. Emm... that the children come out of the school prepared for the challenges that lie ahead. So I don't have any regrets on that (Int. 3, 2007).

Fred recognises that his resilience and sustained commitment would not have been possible without the sacrifices made by his wife and family (Christopher Day and Gu, 2010; Chris. Day, et al., 2007); the personal is key to the ongoing professional identity formation.

Exit Before the Buzz Fades

Fred speculates about when might be the right time to exist the profession, while harbouring the possibility of returning to the African continent, to continue tilting at windmills. He puts this in perspective:

> I'm flying at the moment thanks be to god. We have this plan way back when we came back from Africa that we'd love to go back to work in the third world ... . I'd still like to do that but I don't know how I'm going to get to do it (Int. 3, 2007).

Though not precisely as Fred anticipated, Fred is back in SSA, having retired in August 2010. The teacher and farmer in his persona, his sense of vocation, and giving back, continue to plough new furrows in a new chapter of his life and work. In very recent correspondence, he has intimated missing home, the company of his spouse and the pleasures of a recently arrived grandchild. Perhaps the bachelor farmer within continues to seek challenges?

CONCLUSIONS

I am in agreement with the assertion that 'narrative learning... is... not solely learning *from the narrative*, it is also the learning that goes on in *the act of narration* in the ongoing construction of a life' (Ivor. F. Goodson, Biesta, Tedder, and Adair, 2010, p. 127). However, I want to add that as researcher my learning is both from the narrative as witness and participant in the narration, while there is learning also from the construction of the life history. Fred's story clearly illustrates the manner in which he continues to marshal his 'narrative capital' in the ongoing project of reconstructing a professional persona. When I emailed an earlier version of this chapter to Fred, his initial reaction was: 'this Fred guy should be canonised or as [names wife] would suggest be shot!'—he is both humbled and flattered that his 'story' may have some learning potential for others.

His impulsive response vindicates some considerations on the purposes such narratives may serve in an educational setting. There is ongoing tension between the communicative and autonomous reflexive, perhaps with the latter being more 'blind' to possible learning that would be given more prominence by a communicative reflexive. The story provides evidence that Fred's wife lends a counter balance to his autonomous impulses, as she appears to be more of a communicative reflexive, while there are important gender positionings at play here also. Nevertheless, these inter-personal dynamics add further complexity to the assertion that 'the delicate equation of how life narratives are employed and how narration is processed depends on the balance of learning, identity and agency' (Goodson et al. 2010, p. 129). The life history constructed here provides considerable evidence that Fred is a self-confessed autonomous individual, an impulsive seeker of new challenges. In this regard, Archer suggests that those of this reflexive bent, like Fred, inevitably 'play fast and loose' with constraints since their default positioning appears to be 'being able to capitalise upon enablements and to circumvent constraints' (2007, p. 306). Neither would Fred be likely to dissent from the claim that 'autonomous reflexives are easily prey to boredom at work and champ for greater challenges and more control' (p. 307). It is important to recognise that from a narrative learning perspective, and the achievement of balance that the communicative, autonomous and meta-reflexives be recognised primarily for what they are, their particular way of being in the world. From a professional formation perspective, further work is necessary to gain a greater measure of understanding as to whether or not being more cognisant of the continuum of reflexivity and bringing their distinct elements to the attention of professionals as part of their ongoing re-formation has potential to pay rich learning dividends. I consider that Fred's life history strongly suggests that this is a line of inquiry worth pursuing, while simultaneously recognising that life history method has an important role to play in acknowledging simultaneously personal and professional vulnerabilities and resilience. Paradoxically, these vulnerabilities have potential to be silken threads in the construction of identity narratives while providing continuity and resilience—'keeping a particular narrative going', recognising that the back story continues to be (re-) played in different registers as the life narrative is extended and re-constructed, thus weaving both continuity and change into the very tapestry of the narrative.

NOTES

[1] This particular interview was conducted in his alma mater.

REFERENCES

Archer, M. S. (2000). *Being human the problem of agency*. Cambridge: Cambridge University Press.

Archer, M. S. (2003). *Structure, agency and the internal conversation*. Cambridge: Cambridge University Press.

Archer, M. S. (2007). *Making Our way through the world human reflexivity and social mobility*. Cambridge: Cambridge University Press.

Arnold, B. (2009). *The Irish gulag: How the state betrayed its innocent children*. Dublin: Gill & Macmillan.

Ball, S. (2008). Performativity, privatisation, professionals and the state. In B. Cunningham (Ed.), *Exploring professionalism*, 50–72. London: Institute of Education.

Bauman, Z. (2000/2006). *Liquid modernity* Cambridge: Polity Press.

Britzman, D. (1986). Cultural myths in the making of a teacher: Biography and social structure in teacher education. *Harvard Educational Review, 56*(4), 442–456.

Britzman, D. (1989). Who has the floor: Curriculum teaching and the English teachers struggle for voice. *Curriclum Inquiry, 19*, 143–162.

Britzman, D. (1991). *Practice makes practice a critical study of learning to teach (with a foreword by Maxine Greene)*. New York: SUNY.

Cleary, J. (2007). *Outrageous fortune capital and culture in modern Ireland* (2nd ed.). Dublin: Field Day Publications.

Cooney, J. (1986). *The CROZIER & THE DAIL: Church & State in Ireland1922–1986*. Dublin: The Mercier Press.

Cooper, M. (2009). *Who really runs Ireland? The Story of the elite who led Ireland from bust to boom ... and back again*. Dublin: Penguin Ireland.

Corcoran, M. P., & Peillon, M. (Ed.). (2002). *Ireland unbound: A turn of the century chronicle*. Dublin: Institute of Public Administration.

Day, C., & Gu, Q. (2010). *The new lives of teachers*. London & New York: Routledge.

Day, C., Sammons, P., Stobart, G., Kingston, A., & Gu, Q. (2007). *Teachers matter connecting lives, work and effectiveness*. New York: McGraw Hill and Open University Press.

Denzin, N. K. (2009). *Qualitative inquiry under fire towards a new paradigm dialogue*. Walnut Creek (Ca): Left Coast Press Inc.

Erben, M. (Ed.). (1998). *Biography and education: A reader*. London: Falmer Press.

Giddens, A. (2002). *Runaway world how globalization is reshaping our lives*. London: Profile Books.

Goodson, I. F. (1991). Studying curriculum: a social constructionist perspective. In I. F. Goodson & R. Walker (Eds.) *Biography, Identity & Schooling Episodes in Educational Research*, 168–181. London The Falmer Press.

Goodson, I. F. (2008). *Investigating the teacher's life and work*. Rotterdam/Taipei: Sense Publishers.

Goodson, I. F., & Sikes, P. (Ed.). (2001). *Life history research in educational settings*. Buckingham and Philadelphia: Open University Press.

Goodson, I. F., Biesta, G., Tedder, M., & Adair, N. (2010). *Narrative learning*. London & New York: Routledge.

Hargreaves, D. (1996). *Teaching as a research-based profession: possibilities and prospects*. Paper presented at the annual lecture of the Teacher Training Agency.

Karseth, B. (2011). Teacher education for professional responsibility: What should it look like?. In C. Sugrue & T. Dyrdal Solbrekke (Eds.), *Professional responsibility: New horizons of praxis*. London & New York: Routledge.

Kelchtermans, G. (2011). Professional responsibility: Persistent commitment, perpetual vulnerability? In C. Sugrue & T. Dyrdal Solbrekke (Eds.), *Professional responsibility: New horizons of praxis*. London & New York: Routledge.

Kelchtermans, G., Piot, L., & Ballet, K. (2011). The lucid loneliness of the gatekeeper: Exploring the emotional dimensions in principals' work lives. *Oxford Review of Education*.

MacBeath, J., Gronn, P., Opfer, D., Lowden, K., Forde, C., Cowie, M., et al. (2009). *The Recruitment and retention of headteachers in Scotland (Report to the Scotish Government)*. Edinburgh: The Scottish Government.

McAdams, D. P. (2008). Personal narratives and the life story. In J. Robins & L. A. Pervin (Eds.) *Handbook of personality: Theory and research (3rd edition)*, 242–262. New York: Guilford Press.

O' Connell, M. (2001). *CHANGED UTTERLY Ireland and the new Irish psyche*. Dublin: The Liffey Press.

O' Toole, F. (2009). *Ship of fools how stupidity and corruption sank the Celtic tiger*. London: Faber and Faber.

O' Toole, F. (2010). *Enough is enough: How to build a new republic*. London Faber and Faber.

Polkinghorne, D. E. (1995). Narrative configuration in qualitative analysis. In J. A. Hatch & R. Wisniewski (Eds.) *Life History and Narrative*, 5–24. London: The Falmer Press.

Sugrue, C. (1997). *Complexities of teaching: Child-centred perspectives*. London: Falmer Press.

Sugrue, C. (Ed.). (2005). *Passionate Principalship: Learning from life history of school leaders*. London & New York: Routledge/Falmer.

Sugrue, C., & Furlong, C. (2002). The Cosmologies of Irish primary principals' identities: Between the modern and the post-modern. *International journal of Leadership in Education Theory and Practice, 5*(3), 189–210.

Sugrue, C., & Dyrdal Solbrekke, T. (Eds.). (2011). *Professional responsibility: New horizons of praxis.* London & New York: Routledge.

Taylor, C. (2004/2007) (4th edition). *Modern social imaginaries* Durham & London: Duke University Press.

Wright Mills, C. (1959). *The Sociological imagination.* New York Oxford University Press.

AFFILIATION

Ciaran Sugrue
University College Dublin

10. BODY AND SOUL

A Study of Narratives of Learning Lives of Creative People who Teach

The 'Body and Soul' project is part of a wider narrative of myself as a teacher educator trying to understand the relationship between creativity and teacher knowledge. It written in the context of a popular interest in creativity, immersive focus, finding one's element and developing craft in public discourse (Sennett, 2009, Gladwell, 2009, Robinson, 2010). There is a parallel discourse in teacher education. Current policies for the qualification of teachers in UK mainstream education describe sets of 'standards' for qualification in the education workforce which can promote an instrumental model of learning professionals. These may lose some of the more complex understandings of the ways of knowing that are reflected in the pedagogic relationship between learners and teachers, and the contexts in which they live and work together (TDA, 2007; Putnam and Borko, 2000; Hudson, 2007).

The chapter begins and ends with a personal assertion, written as a reflection at the beginning of my thinking about these themes in 2008; it steps back to explain a theoretical backdrop and then draws upon some themes from the narratives of the learning lives of creative people who teach. Its intention is to make more vivid the concepts of 'depth, scope and reach' in teacher knowledge in these times of challenge and change.

A TEACHER EDUCATOR'S ASSERTION... PART 1

Teachers are people. Their professional knowledge is developed, embodied, and expressed in relationship with other people. As a teacher educator, I am concerned with the education of teachers of the next generation, yet have anxieties about the ways in which strategies and standards can fragment our understanding of knowing and learning as educators. A musician once remarked to me that 'we play as we are' and I understood the resonance with 'we teach as we are'. Our teaching is not just a performance of trained competences to a recognised standard, but an expression of ourselves, our ways of knowing, our cultures and our contexts. I have argued that teaching is a creative endeavour, which involves imagination and value, practice and perseverance, tensions and contradictions. Such a creative endeavour takes place in a dynamic landscape of challenge to the roles of teachers and learners, the shaping of the curriculum, the place of learning environments, and the purposes of formal education.

Ivor F. Goodson, Avril M. Loveless and David Stephens (Eds.), Explorations in Narrative Research, 107–122.

I suggest that it is timely to revisit some of the explorations of teacher identity in this changing landscape, and that we can learn much about teaching and education by turning our gaze to creative educators who work on the margins of our mainstream systems, institutions and learning environments. These educators often work in communities and networks of artists, musicians, artisans, sports players, actors, environmentalists, political activists, development workers, hobbyists, and enthusiasts for topics from archaeology to zymurgy. The mapping of their activity indicates that they work in the contexts of our times, they use tools and technologies to support their activities, and they realise their ideas creatively both in their own practice and in the teaching of others. They may not be formally accredited, but they are recognized in their communities as being teachers in meaningful ways, engaging in reflection, dialogue, human presence, experience, memory and mentorship, and deep understanding of their field.

Origins

The origins of the 'Body and Soul' study lie in observations from many years' experience of research and practice with creative practitioners, working in collaborative projects located in mainstream educational settings (Loveless, 1997; Loveless, 1999a; Loveless, 1999b; Loveless, 2003; Loveless, 2006). The creative practitioners often reflected upon their own subject depth within their particular domains, their contextual scope within wider intellectual, cultural and practice backgrounds, and their pedagogic reach in making connections with learners. Such reflections contrasted with more instrumental models of teaching as delivery of content, strategies and accreditation. They were rooted in creative identities and life trajectories, yet also indicated connections with approaches to learning and pedagogy.

In the reflection above, I recognize a moment when I consciously turned my gaze to creative practitioners. I have always been in the company of troubadours, sign makers and turbulent priests, whilst sitting comfortably in the middle of the mainstream of education institutions such as schools and universities. I wanted to know how to grapple with theory to help describe and explain what it takes to know how to teach—and how to do it well in a complex world.

This chapter doesn't presume to tell the stories of these creative people in any complete way, but recognises how each affords the opportunity to look again at facets of the 'depth, scope and reach' of teacher knowledge. Each person offers a fragment of stories from the margins of the mainstream—an opportunity for me to ask, Raymond Carver-like, 'Where are you calling from?' in order to widen the horizons of the landscape of teacher education.

Why Creative Practitioners?

'Creative practitioners' are people who are identified by themselves and others primarily as creative in a variety of subject domains, from arts to sciences and interdisciplinary collaborations. They are also engaged, from time to time, in roles in education settings, for example as creative partners, mentors, teachers, or coaches. These roles require a pedagogic relationship with learners and the subject domain. The boundaries and range of our learning environments are changing rapidly, and we recognize that there are many people who play significant roles in how and when we learn. Such people might not be qualified teachers in formal educational settings, but demonstrate their depth and scope of understanding in offering substance, support, scaffolding, encouragement and challenge as we learn. Creative practitioners who teach can offer narratives which might 'make the familiar strange' in our understanding of knowledge for education.

Teacher Knowledge, Creativity and Learning

The scene is set against the backdrop of two theoretical fields: knowledge for teacher education, and creativity and learning. Each can be recognized in the European understanding of *Didaktik*—how teacher knowledge is transposed and transformed imaginatively for learners, how didactic analysis and creativity are closely related, and how they are placed in a wider context of *Bildung*, being formed to participate in human society and culture (Loveless, 2011; Klafki, 2000).

Learning to be a teacher is a complex process. Thinking and knowing can be understood as being distributed and situated in social and physical environments which are authentic (see for example: Lave and Wenger, 1991; Wenger, 1998; Salomon, 1993; Putnam and Borko, 2000; Pachler and Daly, 2006). Educators' pedagogical knowledge can be understood as being complex, socio-cultural and conversational (see for example, Leach and Moon, 2008; Loveless and Ellis, 2001; Klafki, 2000; Loveless, 2007b; Shulman and Shulman, 2004; Laurillard, 2008). Teaching can also be described as a creative activity. Teachers express imagination and align their activity with purpose and beliefs. They demonstrate capability in knowing subject domains and how learners learn. They orchestrate appropriate tools and resources, and understand a range of contexts and cultures which reflect the values of education (see for example, Csikszentmihalyi, 1996; Craft et al., 2008; Claxton, 2000; Sternberg and Lubart, 1999; Gardner, 1988; Egan, 2008; Loveless, 2007b; Dillon, 2006; Loveless, 2011).

Formal education in these early years of the 21st century is set in the context of challenges and changes: what we need to know; how we come to know it; where we might learn; which tools for learning we might employ; who might support our learning; and why it might matter to us and to our society. Governments and professional communities engage in debates and consultation on the future of education, curriculum, pedagogy and tools for learning beyond our current horizons, and the understandings of roles and relationships of teachers, learners, knowledge and tools are changing (Cliff et al., 2008; Schuller and Watson, 2009; Alexander, 2009). Fisher et al (2006) call for an approach to teacher learning that is a 'renaissance' rather than a 'retooling'. This would acknowledge teachers as actors in cultural changes in the profession, rather than instruments redesigned when the requirements of the production line change.

Creativity can be described as 'imaginative activity fashioned so as to produce outcomes that are both original and of value' (NACCCE, 1999, p. 29), and as an interaction between characteristics of people and communities, creative processes, subject domains and wider social and cultural contexts (Loveless, 2007a). Previous research has offered a wealth of insights into dimensions of creativity in the context of education. The characteristics of creative practitioners can be recognized in personal qualities of creative individuals, (Sternberg and Lubart, 1999). Gardner presents a pluralist theory of mind which recognises multiple intelligences in individuals (Gardner, 1996). Csikszentmihalyi identifies a common characteristic of creative people as '*flow*'—the automatic, effortless, yet highly focused and engrossed state of consciousness when engaged in activities, often painful, risky or difficult, which stretch a person's capacity whilst involving an element of novelty or discovery (Csikszentmihalyi, 1996). Such states are not just 'letting it flow' or 'leaving it to luck', but acknowledging a way of knowing which is not necessarily conscious, and draws upon resources of knowledge, skill and experience in order to make new combinations, explorations and transformations (Boden, 2001).

Creative practitioners act in social and cultural contexts, and often in collaboration with others (Rhyammar and Brolin, 1999; John-Steiner, 2000; Wix and John-Steiner, 2008; Dillon, 2008). Feldman et al (1994) propose that creativity arises from the interaction between the 'intelligence' of *individuals*, the *domain* or areas of human endeavour, disciplines, crafts or pursuits, and the *field*, such as people, institutions, award mechanisms and 'knowledgeable others' through which judgements of individual performances in society are made.

Creative learning and innovative teaching in mainstream education have been conceptualized in a number of ways, including creative teaching, teaching for creativity and creative learning (Craft, 2005; Jeffrey, 2006; Jeffrey and Woods, 2003; Burnard, 2006; Craft, 2011). In the UK, initiatives such as Creative Partnerships have afforded opportunities and challenges in learners' achievement, teacher development, pedagogy and curriculum reform (Wyse, 2007; Hall et al., 2007; Thomson et al., 2006). In Europe, the strong links between learning and creativity have been explored, indicating the dependence upon context, and the interplay of a number of factors and requisites which can be supported or suppressed within those contexts (Ferrari et al., 2009).

Nevertheless, not much is known about how the learning lives of creative practitioners themselves contribute to learning, practice and pedagogy.

Body and Soul: Introducing the Project Participants

Six creative practitioners were invited to participate in the 'Body and Soul' project in the Spring of 2010. They were known in the community of creative partnerships in schools and universities both for their creative practice within their subject areas, and for their contribution to teaching in different contexts. They were invited to think about learning in their lives, using a timeline of critical events or a drawing as a starting point for discussion if they wished, then engaged in an extended, open interview.

Kima is a visual artist who works in a broad range of media, activities and sites. She declares her interest in the role of the artist within different projects of empowerment such as community or outreach art with studio and collaborative activities. Her teaching includes lecturing in a University Faculty of Arts and Centre for Learning and Teaching in courses of fine art and artists' professional development.

Elliot is an author, illustrator, painter, designer, poet, roller-skater, performer and university lecturer in art and design and creative writing. He draws all these threads of his practice together in the different contexts in which he works, and is currently undertaking doctoral research in 'mavericks' in education.

Sonja is a **playwright** of nearly 20 plays, many performed in the UK, France and Guadeloupe. She writes for general, youth and community audiences and also works as a **writer and drama practitioner** in educational, health and criminal justice settings. Her creative company offers professional development courses for artists and creative practitioners, and she is also a visiting lecturer in university drama schools.

Daniel is a political activist and community worker. He has been involved in the political theatre of direct action for nearly thirty years on national and local scales. His recent activities have focused particularly on the implications of climate change for local contexts. He has involved local communities in creating a community gardens as spaces for leisure and action, as well clean air campaigns and 'bike trains' and 'naked bike rides' for safe riding for groups in traffic-congested areas.

James is a science educator. Now retired from his post as Head of Learning at a prestigious national Museum, he continues his engagement with education with a university Medical School. He has published widely for academic and professional audiences. He has also been a teacher educator and school teacher, focusing on Science, yet renowned amongst his colleagues for approaching his work with a creative sensibility both to the subject and to his pedagogy.

Evan is jazz musician and professor of jazz improvisation in a music conservatoire. Although instructed as a classical performer, jazz improvisation has been the focus of his practice for over thirty years. He composes, performs and records with a wide range of jazz musicians. He also describes himself as an educator, committed to his work with workshops, summer schools, conservatoires and research. He was awarded 'Jazz Educationalist of the Year'.

'Where are you calling from?' Thinking about depth, scope and reach...

In each of the narratives, the relationships between subject focus, pedagogy, and context and purpose, were intertwined around understandings of being creative. The 'depth, scope and reach' of their practice is teased out with selected extracts which offered particular 'narrative intensity' in describing the concept.

Depth

The conceptual depth of educators' understanding relates to the questions of knowledge in subjects domains which identify and debate disciplinary structures, conceptual organizations and principles of enquiry. The participants demonstrated their depth of engagement in, and commitment to their chosen domains whilst recognizing some of the interdisciplinary connections.

Art was not seen as appropriate for an academic pathway for a capable girl, and **Kima** studied linguistics to a high level—yet her 'creative drive' in visual arts was evident from her childhood in her being absorbed in making and shaping things that represented the power of imagination underpinning her ideas.

> I went to Oxford and I took languages, and then nearly became an academic in German. And then turned everything around, chucked it all in and went to art school, did a second degree. So, you know, the rest is history... I like the word drive, I think it was just really that there was this... there was this creative drive which, as you say, didn't go away.

> I kind of make things in my mind out of clay, if not actually in reality... It pleased me to see that I could make things, that, you know, that I could make things well and I enjoyed that.

> Playing around with the truth. I was inventing... So I remember telling a friend at school that, that we had six white horses and we kept them at the bottom of the garden... But, um, it's, it's something I still have a kind of, um, a sort of liking for, although of course now it's called art and invention and imagination, so it's not a kind of a problem, actually. But there's... some kind of association going on between kind of using your imagination and telling untruths, which, which is kind of a bit, kind of complicated. I suppose what I was doing at the time was I was kind of learning about, you know, the, the power of the imagination and how you can invent things, and that that has consequences, you know. So, say a responsibility kind of comes in. And I feel that very strongly as an artist that, you know, if I'm going to make something, put it out into the world, then I want to think very carefully about what that is...

> I suppose my approach is, as I said, that, that these ideas pop up in my head, and often they're... often they're finished. I can see something finished in my mind... And then it's a matter of bringing it out, so externalising it somehow, and that's kind of the difficult bit. Lately I've had a few pieces of work made by other people because they've required skills that I don't have. It's not that satisfying somehow. So maybe that's another way... so maybe things either come ready-made into my mind, and I have to make them, get them out, or get somebody to help me to make them and externalise them, or, or else they're things which come about through conversation, dialogue, discussion, some kind of creative friction...

I mean I said before that you shouldn't call yourself an artist unless you're actually making art. I've kind of claimed it for myself, I suppose over the years because I sort of see it as a job and I think it involves a way of thinking which is questioning and inventive and creative and playful and all of those things which I like, really, and a bit... a bit rebellious and a bit hard to pin down. So I like all those things.

James' account of his engagement with science education reflected his approach to being a scientist, with an interdisciplinary understanding, and the subject being 'actually a human activity'.

Because my natural thinking is very much cross-curricular, although I'm passionate about science education, I don't see that as an isolated area of learning... Start with a real-life situation; look at what it is you really want to find out about, within that. Try and do that finding out, and then, make sense of it theoretically afterwards. Which, after all, is the way that the real world does science, but that's not necessarily seen as very sensible in the circles in which I've been moving for the last 40 years.

It seemed to me that it would make a lot more sense if we took the analytic approach and therefore linked things together—certainly within subject domains, but, wherever possible, outside and beyond. I think, one of the things that struck me was, even within science, the discovery of the structure and operation of DNA, back in the 50s, was made because people from very disparate areas of science worked together, and therefore, their output was much greater than if they'd been working individually, on their own separate areas of interest. That always struck me, in retrospect, as really quite powerful, rather than the atomized way that we were approaching stuff. Interestingly, as a by-the-by, that paper in Nature, of the structure of DNA, I've used for many year, as an example of demolishing myths, the myth of science as a neutral subject. I think that's important too. The reason that I use it for that is, it begins with the word 'we'. 'We wish to announce the structure for DNA'—not 'the structure for DNA has been discovered', which is the way one was always taught to write about science. I think that probably I'd always appreciated that somehow, that science was actually a human activity and therefore had scope for people to be imaginative and creative and it wasn't simply the revelation of truth by some dull, systematic approach, even though there are dull, repetitive, systematic bits, and I think that was... that dimension, somehow... in retrospect. I think that if you'd asked to 20 years ago, what I was doing and why, I would have found it rather more difficult to articulate...

Scope

An educators' 'contextual scope' is their awareness of their relationship to other people, ways of knowing, culture, politics and power within a wider context. They know where they fit—or not—in the landscape, and why what they do might matter and have value. Contextual scope is related to the 'Why?' questions in the Didaktik tradition, reflected in the relationship between knowing a subject and being human.

Daniel described his learning life as engaged in direct action which embodied the issues of protest and change, spanning a period of over twenty years. His creative practice is related to imaginative approaches to direct action as theatre and community art forms which challenge power and promote participation by drawing on traditions of performing protest. His approach integrates the personal, political, local and global dimensions of this activity and he describes 'the learning is in the doing of it'.

> I think very significant for me, in terms of my learning; in terms of how my life has been as an adult, has been going to university; studying Social Sciences. But I think a lot of the learning opportunities that came up around that, rather than in the curriculum, the extra-curricular activities which were very vibrant at Sussex University in the 80s; probably still are. So, getting involved in making videos; getting involved in making radio programmes; being in the politics of that era, talking early eighties really, the Thatcher era and the student response to that, which was very, very active and vociferous. Also very important in the politics at that time, was the Peace Movement, which was huge; the cruise missiles coming to the UK, at Greenham Common; the Conservative Government at the time, going ahead, deciding to invest in more nuclear weapons in the form of Trident Missiles. So there was a huge protest, very creative protest culture around that that I started to get involved with as well. I'd always been committed to those issues, but I think part of the politics and the mood at the university at that time, was to engage in those issues very strongly. Also the Women's Movement was very, very active at that time... which I think both informed me in terms of how the personal is political, that kind of idea which was very big in the Women's Movement at that time. And I think, is something that carries on today, really, that idea.

> .... being creative, being fun, being colourful, being funny; challenging authority in a different way; going around the side, rather than going head-on ... and that kind of huge tradition that they represented of political struggle... So I think that's a very effective way of engaging a wider audience, not just a politician's, but engaging the public in understanding the issues and thinking about issues. Justice is done on a stage... Always keep it friendly. Keep it assertive. Maintain integrity. Be the change you want to see, those kinds of things. So to embody the message in the way we would protest.

> I think of course, there's a very strong tradition of all of those things that come from or are affected by the Civil Rights Movement in America, in the sixties; the Suffragette Movement in Britain, and even the Aldermaston Marches to some extent. There was a Direct Action movement in the sixties that had come out of that. So there were very much those influences that were a part of our culture, really. There's Ghandi, of course, and those kind of

iconic non-violent struggles, and I think those methods and techniques have been woven into what happened in the eighties, and what's happening now, really. But I think it's a very rich tradition that continually reinvents itself, and engages new people all the time, and engages with new issues and uses those techniques, but always new ideas to use.

The learning is in the doing of it.

Elliot placed the story of his learning life clearly in the context of his early, sometimes critical experiences of not conforming at school, yet having a supportive family. He recognised some of the connections between these experiences and his abilities as an artist and teacher. He spoke of his 'walking against the grain'. Becoming a Christian had a significant effect on his life and relationships, and he describes Christ as 'the ultimate maverick and a great teacher'.

As I hated school, I had to find the learning somewhere else... I lived in my own world for 14 years... Ah, but I created my own world and became very inventive. But fortunately there was one teacher and I think that we often identify people that switch the lights on in our heads... He would offer you the learning with his own inspiration and enthusiasm and we would do lots of topics... So I would go to Majorca and do my topic on Majorca and when there I would seek out the culture. I'd sit down and I'd learn to draw, and water colour pencils had just been invented... I've only got one remaining example of a painting that I did at the age of ten. That's all that's left, and interestingly, it's of a scene in Majorca around a bay, very much the sort of thing that I'd still go and do now, even the composition's about the same, ability is different. And I think bringing that back and putting that together with the words in a topic situation was vital to my learning at that time. That meant the world to me doing that sort of thing.

So my aversion to school, ah, was because basically it wasn't suiting me. Um, I kind of slipped quite heavily and I became branded as very silly boy in my education because I started writing my own comics, loosely based on Monty Python. I opened up an entrepreneurial business from a lock-up, called—I'm sorry to have to say this—Vomit Products... I was recording my own music, ah, I was doing four track recording and I was speeding my voice up by, by taking two batteries out of the cassette recorder and putting a piece of wire over it. It actually slowed the reels so it speeded up my voice and then I'd track that. And I was drumming inside washing machines to get echoes and highly inventive stuff, I think. I, I say to my children when they ask me about this, I say, you know, it's one of the most creative times of my life, and it was really important.

There were some glimmers of hope there. [One of the teachers] was a great technician, artistic technician... He knew his stuff. He knew his art history and he had a passion for it... By the way, I'm still in touch with all of these people. It's quite important because they are links to my education. I have credited them with books. There are books dedicated to these people because I think it's really important that that is maintained.

[On the timeline of his teens] did I write conversion to Christianity?... This is major... I reckoned it was going to cost everything because that's what I was told but I'd looked at that and I realized there was something attractive about Christ and this person, whether this person was truly alive, whether there is a God or not, I liked the idea of the life, and I liked what was being said again—Christ the ultimate maverick and a great teacher. I realize that now. Didn't then... You see there's something anti in me that will always walk against the grain... I'd always walk against the tide and I still do. And this Christianity offered something against the tide... Things changed almost overnight and suddenly I was serious about things and I started to sort of turn things around.

But, I just keep going, you know, because you can't be what you're—you can't become what you're not. You've got to be who you are. If it's in you to be creative, what else are you going to do?... I know I'm subversive, and I'm proud of that... I live with the tensions, that are the liminality.

Reach...

'Reach' describes the ways in which educators make pedagogic connections with learners. This might be through the pedagogic content knowledge, the transposition and transformation of subject knowledge appropriate for learners. It is also through the repertoire of pedagogic strategies which teachers employ when they are 'ready, willing and able' to teach.

Sonja describes the writing process as a way of responding to and understanding the world ('processing, processing, processing'). She perceives that the creative and educating dimensions of her work as having become almost indistinguishable. She worked with 'The Theatre of the Oppressed' and the principle of using creativity to create change through work with groups in the community. She asserts 'the power of creativity to change lives' and suggests the term 'amateur' as an alternative to 'educator'.

... so that's the mid-eighties that I date my, almost, two things of being an artist and then an educator; that I developed these two strands, and they started crossing over, as well, from then. And they do become almost indistinguishable, I think...

I'm modelling it anyway. I think that my approach to learning and teaching is about facilitating and enabling people to reflect on their own work, their own practice, where they've come from, and think what they already know, and then to develop that.

The traditional view of education is a brick wall of knowledge that you add to bit by bit, whereas I think what I do is a different thing, all about making connections and seeing things in a different way and suddenly going 'ooh—that bit over there and then that bit over there, which is the same thing—if I—put them together, something else happens'. And that is a different educational process… different learning process.

I think it is interesting that, having said I don't want to be a teacher, I've finished up teaching, in inverted commas. You ask people why you want to do this work, and they quite often say they want to give something back, or that they felt that sense of being not quite at ease and wanting to make it better for other people. And I think that's quite an interesting driving force, actually… But I wouldn't call myself a teacher. Am I contradicting myself there? I don't think I would. I would say I was a facilitator, or an educator, possibly. But I wouldn't say a teacher. Educator? Educator is quite a loaded word, actually. An amateur. Well, now that I'm thinking about it [the word educator]… In the traditional sense of drawing out, I would agree with that—yes.

Evan considers reflection on pedagogy as an integral part of his practice as a musician and educator. He described tools for preparing to teach, from lesson planning to teaching strategies and reflection, and he honoured the role of mentors in his own learning. He spoke of the relationship between knowing in a domain such as music, and the role of discipline as understood in a spiritual practice.

I'm always interested in how people learn and how they practise, so I'm frequently saying as soon as you know how to practise your relationship changes with the art form and with the teachers—and the teachers become, it becomes less vertical and the teacher becomes more the mentor and less of a transmitter of knowledge … My philosophical view is I would like to be able to enable the students to become the musician they want to become, not a projection of the musician I am.

I can teach in a very dynamic way and I mean I can be quite charismatic when I teach and I deliberately don't, you know. I really often make a point of trying to reduce my physical status you know—well I often deliberately sit down and I'll let the students think longer than they're comfortable with sometimes—and erm when L was doing this work last year she observed some teaching. She wasn't shocked, but she was surprised at the lengths, the discipline I went through to not intrude on the students' experience.

… I mean I discovered that a lot of what I thought was student-centred isn't necessarily student-centred. I think I was confusing experiential learning and improvising for student-centeredness. I think the presence of experiential learning and improvising means that there is a high degree of student-centredness, or student control and autonomy, but you can still have open and closed questions within those situations—and closed questions are owned by the teacher or the subject area.

... part of me thinks that if somebody's in touch with their vocation...and education is to do with their vocation, then I think somehow they evoke a special relationship with their—it's no longer a subject area, it's something profound and beyond that, much more to do with a sense of being... it is vital, literally vital, and I think that redefines the relationship with the students.

I want the students to be energized by the learning experience, rather than the teacher... your learning will be how you negotiate how you use the ideas that you encounter or make sense of... Maybe having to negotiate those things every day maybe quite a good thing for your mind and your soul. I don't know if people teaching French in an inner city school on Thursday afternoons get the same kick we do teaching improvisation, but maybe there's something in the model that might be useful. Yeah, I think improvisation is good for you.

Narratives of 'Body and Soul'

These fragments of narratives contribute to the thematic description of 'depth, scope and reach' in creative practice and pedagogy, yet within each fragment there are connections and echoes of the others, as each of the six narratives could have contributed to all of the themes. The depth of conceptual understanding of the subject domain is woven in the fabric of people's cultural, historical and personal life. There is a mutual shaping of domain and identity as human activity in context (Holland et al., 1998, Cole, 1996). There are profound connections for these people between being creative and being an educator. Depth, scope and reach are embodied in their pedagogy, which resonates with the principles of their mastery and ways of knowing (Eisner, 1985). The seeming paradox of their creative pedagogy is that improvisation in the pedagogic moments requires practice in concepts and context (Loveless, 2007b).

How does a narrative research approach contribute to an understanding of teacher knowledge which reflects a complex and holistic understanding of content, purpose and pedagogy? Narratives offer not only vivid illustration of emergent themes, but illumination into intentional states and the reasons that underpin people's choices, actions and relationships (Bruner, 1996). These narratives of creative people who teach, speak of agency and power as they tell the stories of their learning and creative lives, drawing upon curiously old-fashioned concepts such as 'vocation', 'discipline', 'tradition', 'amateur', 'practice' and 'drive'. The narratives offer not only the 'familiar' themes of creative fashioning and flow, but also the 'strangeness' of their particular biographies and niches. The depth, scope and reach of these educators are grounded and generative, substantial and shared. Their narratives give glimpses of embodiment and wholeheartedness in creative practice shared in their teaching. Such narratives contribute to my own narrative as a teacher educator seeking understanding by paying attention to the margins of my own context.

The landscape of teacher education in England is changing—again. The challenges are not local, but entwined in the global changes in economies and markets, in neo-liberal politics, in social structures, in social democracy and in power. The experience of these changes is, however, very personal. The choreography of the so-called craft of teaching is breathtaking complex, enormously demanding and requires partnerships between many people with knowledge of subject, context and learning.

Narratives of depth, scope and reach can be used as 'writerly texts', provoking hearers into creating their own (Barthes 1985 in Bruner, 1996). Saunders reminds us that 'the researcher's and poet's responsibility, and talent, is not just to 'tell it like it is' but to add a deeper sounding'(2003, p. 185). We need understanding not only how to teach fractions, phonics and triple science from leafy suburbs to urban estates, but also how the narrative capital of individuals practising to some purpose within communities might contribute to being a teacher in our times.

A TEACHER EDUCATOR'S ASSERTION... PART II

We can learn from them, through creative conversations, narrative, and research methods which resonate with their fields and the questions that they ask about the things that matter to them. They can offer insights into their expertise, integrity, ways of knowing, relationship with others, commitment to process and substance. They can demonstrate how to embody being a teacher for different purposes, in different environments, and in different situations from one-to-one encounters, group work, teams, master classes, whole classroom teaching, to communicating online. They can offer, not models of learning objectives in 'informal learning' or 'beyond the school', but alternative views of being a teacher outside the usual institutions and professions. Such creative conversations can help us to think again about the identities of teachers and contribute to a more radical charting of the landscape of teacher education. We need critical, creative teachers who are prepared not only to deal with what is, but are also sustained in asking questions, envisioning alternatives, embodying praxis, and reading the world with political awareness of their professional identity and agency.

REFERENCES

Alexander, R. (Ed.) (2009). *Children, their world, their education: Final report and recommendations of the Cambridge Primary Review*. London: Routledge.

Bruner, J. (1996). *The culture of education*. Cambridge, MA: Harvard University Press.

Burnard, P. (2006). Reflecting on the creativity agenda in education. *Cambridge Journal of Education, 36*, 313–318.

Claxton, G. (2000). The anatomy of intuition. In T. Atkinson & G. Claxton (Eds.) *The intuitive practitioner*. Buckingham, Philadelphia: Open University Press.

Cliff, D., O'Malley, C., & Taylor, J. (2008). Beyond current horizons: Future issues in socio-technical change in education. Bristol: Futurelab & DCSF.

Cole, M. (1996). *Cultural psychology: A once and future discipline*. Cambridge, MA: Harvard University Press.

Craft, A. (2005). *Creativity in schools: Tensions and dilemmas*. London: Routledge.

Craft, A. (2011). *Creativity and education futures in the digital age*. Stoke On Trent: Trentham Books.

Craft, A., Claxton, G., & Gardner, H. (Eds.) (2008). *Creativity, wisdom, and trusteeship*. Thousand Oaks, California: Corwin Press.

Csikszentmihalyi, M. (1996). *Creativity: flow and the psychology of discovery and invention*. New York: HarperCollins.

Dillon, P. (2006). Creativity, integrativism and a pedagogy of connection. *Thinking Skills and Creativity, 1*, 69–83.

Dillon, P. (2008). Creativity, wisdom and trusteeship—Niches of cultural production. In A. Craft, H. Gardner & G. Claxton (Eds.) *Creativity, wisdom and trusteeship in education*. Thousand Oaks, CA: Corwin Press.

Egan, K. (2008). *The future of education: Reimagining our schools from the ground up*. New Haven and London: Yale University Press.

Eisner, E. W. (1985). Aesthetic modes of knowing. *84th Yearbook of the national society for the study of education: Learning and teaching the ways of knowing*. Chicago IL: University of Chicago Press.

Feldman, D. H. (1994). Creativity: Proof that development occurs. In D. H. Feldman, M. Csikszentrnihalyi & H. Gardner Changing the world: A framework for the study of creativity. Westport, Conn: Praeger, pp. 85–102.

Ferrari, A., Cachia, R., & Punie, Y. (2009). Innovation and creativity in education and training in the EU member states: Fostering creative learning and supporting innovative teaching. Literature review on innovation and creativity in E&T in the EU Member States (ICEAC). European Commission, Joint Research Centre, Institute for Prospective Technological Studies.

Fisher, T., Higgins, C., & Loveless, A. (2006). Teachers learning with digital technologies: A review of research and projects. Bristol: Futurelab.

Gardner, H. (1988). Creative lives and creative works: A Synthetic scientific approach. In R. J Sternberg (Ed.) *The nature of creativity*. New York: Cambridge University Press.

Gladwell, M. (2009). *Outliers: The story of success*. London: Penguin.

Hall, C., Thomson, P., & Russell, L. (2007). Teaching like an artist: The pedagogic identities and practices of artists in schools. *British Journal of Sociology of Education, 28*, 605–619.

Holland, D., Lachicotte, W., Skinner, D., & Cain, C. (1998). *Identity and agency in cultural worlds*. Cambridge, Massachusetts and London, England: Harvard University Press.

Hudson (2007). Comparing different traditions of teaching and learning: What can we learn about teaching and learning? *European Educational Research Journal, 6*, 135–146.

Jeffrey, B. (Ed.) (2006). *Creative learning practices: European experiences*, London, Tufnell Press.

Jeffrey, B. & Woods, P. (2003). *The creative school: A framework for success, quality and effectiveness*. London & New York: Routledge, Falmer.

John-Steiner, V. (2000). *Creative collaboration*. New York: Oxford University Press.

Klafki, W. (2000). Didaktik analysis as the core of preparation of instruction. In I. Westbury, S. Hopmann, & K. Riquarts (Eds.) *Teaching as a reflective practice: The German didaktik tradition*. Mahwah: Lawrence Erlbaum Associates.

Laurillard, D. (2008). The teacher as action researcher: Using technology to capture pedagogic form. *Studies in Higher Education, 33*, 139–154.

Lave, J., & Wenger, E. (1991). *Situated learning*. Legitimate peripheral participation. Cambridge: Cup.

Leach, J., & Moon, B. (2008). *The power of pedagogy*. Los Angeles, London: New Delhi, Singapore, Sage.

Loveless, A. (1997). Visual literacy and new technology in primary schools: The Glebe School project. *Journal of Computing and Childhood Education, 8*, 98–110.

Loveless, A. (1999a). A digital big breakfast: The Glebe School project. In Sefton-Green, J. (Ed.) *Young people, creativity and new technology: The challenge of digital arts*. London, Routledge.

Loveless, A. (1999b). Art on the net evaluation – a report to South East Arts, Lighthouse and DCMS. Brighton: University Of Brighton.

Loveless, A. (2003). Making a difference? An evaluation of professional knowledge and pedagogy In art and ICT. *International Journal of Art and Design Education, 22*, 145–154.

Loveless, A. (2006). ICT and arts education—for art's sake? In C. Crawford (Ed.) *International Society for Information Technology in Teacher Education.* Orlando, Florida, USA: Association for the Advancement of Computers in Education.

Loveless, A. (2007a). Creativity, technology and learning: A review of recent literature (Update). Bristol: Futurelab.

Loveless, A. (2007b). Preparing to teach with ICT: Subject knowledge, didaktik and improvisation. *The Curriculum Journal,* 18.

Loveless, A. (2011). Didactic analysis as a creative process: Pedagogy for creativity with digital tools. In B. Hudson & M. A. Meyer (Eds.) *Beyond fragmentation: Didactics, learning and teaching in Europe.* Opladen and Farmington Hills: Verlag Barbara Budrich

Loveless, A. & Ellis, V. (Eds.) (2001). *ICT, pedagogy and the curriculum: Subject to change.* London: Routledge.

NACCCE (1999). All our futures: Creativity, culture and education. Sudbury: National Advisory Committee on Creative and Cultural Education: DfEE And DCMS.

Pachler, N., & Daly, C. (2006). Professional teacher learning in virtual environments. *E-Learning, 3*, 62–74.

Putnam, R. T., & Borko, H. (2000). What do new views of knowledge and thinking have to say about research on teacher learning? *Educational Researcher, 29*, 4–15.

Rhyammar, L., & Brolin, C. (1999). Creativity research: Historical considerations and main lines of development. *Scandinavian Journal of Educational Research, 43*, 259–273.

Robinson, K. (2010). *The element: How finding your passion changes everything.* London: Penguin.

Salomon, G. (1993). *Distributed cognitions: Psychological and educational considerations.* Cambridge: Cambridge University Press.

Saunders, L. (2003). On flying, writing poetry and doing educational research. *British Educational Research Journal, 29*, 175–187.

Schuller, T., & Watson, D. (2009). Learning through life: inquiry into the future for lifelong learning (IFLL). Leicester, National Institute of Adult Continuing Education.

Sennett, R. (2009). *The craftsman.* London: Penguin.

Shulman, L. S., & Shulman, J. H. (2004). How and what teachers learn: A shifting perspective. *Journal of Curriculum Studies, 36*, 257–271.

Sternberg, R. J., & Lubart, T. I. (1999). The concept of creativity: Prospects and paradigms. In R. J Sternberg (Ed.) *Handbook of Creativity.* Cambridge, UK: Cambridge University Press.

TDA (2007). The revised standards for the recommendation for qualified teacher status (QTS). Training and development agency for schools.

Thomson, P., Hall, C., & Russell, L. (2006). An arts project failed, censored or...? A critical incident approach to artist-school partnerships. *Changing English, 13*, 29–44.

Wenger, E. (1998). Communities of practice: Learning, meaning and identity. Cambridge: Cambridge University Press.

Wix, L., & John-Steiner, V. (2008). Peer-Enquiry: Discovering what you know through dialogue. *Thinking skills and creativity, 3*, 217–225.

Wyse, D. (2007). Partners in creativity: Action research and creative partnerships. *Education 3–13, 35*, 181–191.

AFFILIATION

Avril Loveless
University of Brighton

11. TRUTHS, TRUTHS AND TREATING PEOPLE PROPERLY

Ethical Considerations for Researchers who use Narrative and Auto/Biographical Approaches

INTRODUCTION

Researching, writing about and re-presenting lives carries a heavy ethical burden. This is the case regardless of whatever methodology, specific data collection methods, or presentational styles are adopted. For those who choose to use narrative and/or auto/biographical approaches however, ethical issues and questions around truth are often more obvious, immediate and challenging than they are for researchers working within other traditions and using other strategies. This is because individual and specific people, their various and varying roles, relationships, identities, experiences, perceptions, aims and motivations are central both to all aspects of the research endeavour and to the substantive focus of that research. As a result, and compared with investigations which seek to generalise rather than to concentrate on the particular, the consequences of unethical research and writing practices on the part of auto/biographical and narrative researchers can be more immediate and personal and indeed ultimately may be more damaging (see Adams, 2008, p. 183). I agree with Laurel Richardson that 'narrativising, like all intentional behaviour... is a site of moral responsibility' (1990, p. 131) and in this chapter my aim is to raise some of the ethical issues inherent in the relationships between epistemology, methodology, theory generation, re-presentation and truth as they currently relate to narrative and auto/biographical social science research and writing (see also Sikes, 2010a). As well as looking at the ethical responsibility of the researcher with regard to research participants, I will also consider the researcher/writer's responsibilities to their readers with respect to any claims they may make to be advancing knowledge/truths about the social world. My aim is to provoke thinking and discussion rather than to provide any definitive answers.

Taking this line is not a 'cop out', but rather, my intention is to emphasise and reflect that every research situation is contextually and historically located and that, as Richard Pring (2000) points out, each generates its own singular and idiosyncratic ethical questions and issues that demand specific and situational consideration, drawing on the perspectives that the different approaches to and conceptualisations of ethics offer (see Sikes, 2010a). I also want to argue that different people coming from different positions with different biographies may well see things differently and could reach different conclusions about what

Ivor F. Goodson, Avril M. Loveless and David Stephens (Eds.), Explorations in Narrative Research, 123–140.

constitutes ethical practice, although all may be able to offer a convincing justification for their view.

At this point I must make it clear that, for me, in a research context (and in any other context for that matter, because even a shopping list tells a story) if I'm writing, I'm engaged in crafting a narrative. Furthermore I consider all of the writing that we may do in connection with any research project to be both narrative re-presentation and an integral component of that research. I see writing and the construction of narrative as a method of inquiry (Richardson, 1994) and when I talk about 'research' or 'writing' the chances are that I will be using the terms to mean the same overall practice. I am not, here, going to be going in to great detail around the nature and definition of auto/biographical or narrative enquiry. These are areas which have provoked considerable discussion and debate which can be pursued elsewhere. My view is that if someone believes themselves to be engaging in these kinds of research they probably are. What is important though is that they make it absolutely clear as to what they are doing, why and how they are doing it and why they consider their research to be what they claim it is.

AN AUTO/BIOGRAPHICAL AND NARRATIVE APPROACH

In keeping with the title and focus of this chapter I have decided to take an approach which is explicitly auto/biographical and narrative. Over the years since 1978 when I simultaneously began my career as an educational researcher and discovered that I agreed with W. I. Thomas and Florian Znaniecki—that 'life records constitute the *perfect* type of sociological material' (1918–1920, p. 1831), I have spent much time thinking and writing about the relationship between 'truth', ethics, epistemology, methodology, theorising and re-presentation and the ways in which they interact. A review of what I have had to say around these concerns at various times (eg. Goodson and Sikes, 2001; Measor and Sikes, 1992; Sikes, 1986, 1997, 2000, 2006a, 2009 2010a, 2010b; Sikes and Goodson, 2003; Sikes, Measor and Woods, 1985; Sikes and Piper, 2010a, 2011) reveals that, despite fundamental similarities, there are differences, albeit often slight. Sometimes these differences can be attributed to such things as: the substantive focus of the particular research I'm writing about; decisions I may have made about what I want to emphasise; the type and nature of the publication a piece of writing is appearing in; or to editorial direction. However, each time I need to write about these types of issues (and because of the sort of work I do, that is relatively frequently) I try to come to the task anew and afresh and every time I return it is in an iterative reflexive and reflective way, influenced and informed by personal—auto/biographical experiences and consequent learning and knowledge gained in the interim (see Sikes and Goodson, 2003; Stanley, 1993; contributors to White Riley, 1988). Tony Adams and Stacy Holman Jones write about 'deja-vu prose that makes the familiar hum with newness' (2011, p. 108) and writing this chapter has been for me, once again, an example of this kind of exercise.

Histories and Fashions

Alongside the auto/biographical influences on my thinking there is also an historical contextual dimension to the differences which is rooted in contemporary trends and preoccupations and in evolving and changing beliefs and values within the wider social setting in general and in specific research related communities in particular (see Denzin and Lincoln, 2005; Lincoln and Denzin, 2005). Scientific, technological and moral 'revolutions' (Appiah, 2010), zeitgeist style changes or fashions in research (see Flyvbjerg, 2001; Sikes, 2009) lead to changes in how we make sense of the world as a whole, occasioning shifts in the philosophical, epistemological, methodological and axiological perspectives and understandings underlying and informing research *per se*. Thus how we think about and variously address such questions and issues as:

- That can be considered to be legitimate 'research';
- How researchers' values and life experiences influence their work;
- That constitutes ethical research practice;
- That forms can research re-presentation take and still be considered social science 'research';
- That is a true account and is such a thing possible;
- That are the relationships between and the ethical responsibilities of researchers/writers and the people whose lives are the focus and substance of research/writing.

This, I believe, a personal and a collective (Deleuzian) becoming and therefore continuous, project.

On the basis of this view I am going to offer some narrative reflections, vignettes which tell stories drawing on experiences that I have had—as a researcher, as a supervisor of students' research, as an ethics reviewer, as an examiner of doctoral theses and as a peer reviewer and reader of journal papers—which have something to say about ethics and truth in auto/biographical and narrative research.

ETHICAL REVIEW PROCEDURES AND THE QUEST FOR ETHICAL RESEARCH PRACTICE

The stories I am going to tell are, essentially, stories from the field, research narratives which I am going to use as illustrative data even though they were not collected as part of a planned and pre-defined research project. In this they are much like narratives taken from lives lived long before the researcher came along as they would be in a life history project or, in the case of autoethnography, before someone decided to turn a 'scientific' gaze upon their own experiences. Should I, therefore, seek ethical clearance from the committee at my university before I write and tell them?

These days this is an important question yet, in the context of the UK, a decade ago (and even more recently in many institutions) it would have been very unlikely to have been asked. The whole area of formalised ethical review of social science research is something which, although relatively new, has had a significant and pervasive effect on what is researched and how research is conducted. It has also had implications for researcher identity in that it affects conceptualisations of what 'ethical researchers' do (Tierney and Blumberg Corwin, 2007). There is a large and growing body of literature which is critical of the reasons for ethical review and of the ways in, and extent to, which procedures have been imposed upon the social sciences. Kevin Haggarty (2004), for instance, talks of 'ethics creep' and Mark Israel and Ian Hay speak for many when they suggest that:

> social scientists are angry and frustrated. They believe their work is being constrained and distorted by regulators of ethical practice who do not understand social science research. In the United States, Canada, the United Kingdom, New Zealand and Australia, researchers have argued that regulators are acting on the basis of biomedically driven arrangements that make little or no sense to social scientists (2006, p. 1).

The anger and frustration is more keenly felt because, as Martyn Hammersley has pointed out, there is no evidence to suggest that there is or has been 'substantial unethical behaviour on the part of social scientists which would justify such a lack of trust' (Hammersley, 2009, p. 217–218).

However, whilst there may be no large scale ethical social science research scandals to compare with the likes of the Tuskagee Syphilis in the Negro Male and the Alder Hey Organ Retention scandals (see Sikes, & Piper, 2010b, p. 206–207) controversies such as those surrounding Wilfred Foote Whyte's (1943) *Street Corner Society* study (see Boelen, 1992; Whyte, 1992) and Carolyn Ellis' (1986) *Fisher Folk* research (see Ellis, 1995 and 2007; Tolich, 2004) show that people can and do experience harm as a result of participating in projects which have narrative and/or auto/biographical elements. The extent to which ethical review procedures can prevent harm happening is, however, another matter (although I am not going to be going into these arguments here, see Sikes and Piper, 2011 for a review) and indeed, some authors have argued that formalised, one size fits all, blanket procedures can, in themselves lead to unethical practice (see for example Allen, Anderson, Bristol, Downs, O'Neill, Watts and Wu, 2009; Cannella and Lincoln, 2007; Halse and Honey, 2007; Lincoln, 2005; Lincoln and Cannella, 2009; Macfarlane, 2009; Sikes and Piper 2010b).

Authorial Honesty

Since I am claiming that what I am going to say is based on my experiences, I have to ask readers to trust that this is indeed the case. With reference to the relationship between reader and writer Ron Pelias suggests that 'there are certain kinds of contractual obligations you evoke with certain types of genre' (personal communication reported in Tullis Owen, McRae, Adams and Vitale 2009, p. 189). Laurel Richardson elaborates on a similar theme when she notes that:

> claiming to write 'fiction' is different from claiming to write 'science' in terms of the audience one seeks, the impact one might have on different

publics, and how one expects 'truth claims' to be evaluated. These differences should not be overlooked or minimised (2000, p. 926).

Central to what Pelias and Richardson are saying here is the notion that authorial honesty is important. This is not to say that there is not a place for fiction in social science writing. I entirely agree with Mike Angrossino that 'a story doesn't have to be factual in order to be true' (1998, p. 34) and with Margaret Attwood that 'a thing can be true, but not true, but true nonetheless' (2008, p. 3). However, if we are going to use fiction, metaphor, allegory or some other conceit, my view is that we should be clear that we are doing this with the aim of, for instance, evoking a sense of feel, place, empathy or understanding, or to encourage readers to question their taken for granted assumptions.

Seeking to re-present the myriad perspectives or, in other words, the personal and shared truths that characterise human understanding of any and every social situation or life experience, is what narrative and auto/biographical researchers/writers are about. This quest, I believe, involves acknowledging both 'the inevitable gaps between reality, experience and expression' (Moen, 2006, p. 63–64) and also that the life as told or otherwise depicted is not, and never can be, the life as lived (see Bruner 1993, p. 38–39). It also means, I would suggest, that if we make any sort of truth claims there is a responsibility to be honest about the routes we have taken to arrive at them. Referring to Gary Fine's point that ethnographic writing is typically 'accepted on faith' (1993, p. 269) Julian Tullis Owen *et al* comment that 'no one questions the 'recreated conversations' we produce from interviews, but questioning could occur if we claim to have conducted and transcribed conversations' (2009, p. 181). Indeed.

Truths, Truths and the Protection of People Involved in Research

My first job was as a research assistant working on the SSRC/Gulbenkian project, *The Problems and Effects of Teaching about Race Relations* (Stenhouse, Verma, Wild and Nixon, 1982). The project had collected audio recordings of hundreds of hours of classroom discussion, and also some student writing, about aspects of 'race' relations (in the terminology of the time). My task was to review these materials and select excerpts for a text (Sikes, 1979) to be used in CPD (Continuing Professional Development) for teachers working in this difficult and controversial field. One day I came across an essay that demonstrated the power narrative accounts have both to evoke 'empathetic scholarship' (Pelias, 2004) and to provoke the sort of sociological imagination (Mills, 1970) that can lead to transformative action. It also raised questions about truth and truths and about the protection of people involved in research.

The Most Terrifying Experience I've Had

The most terrifying experience I have had took place last year from early September to late December but it was also one of the best times in my life. The cause of this was the announcement made by the President of Uganda,

His Excellency, Amyn Dada, saying that all non-Ugandan Asians should leave Uganda in ninety days. The result was that twenty eight thousand came to Britain, more than ten thousand went to Canada and the rest, save for about a hundred went to United Nation camps in foreign countries or to neighbouring countries. I myself, am a Ugandan citizen but as my parents hold British passports, I was given visas for entering and settling in Britain. Although my father's intention was to come to Britain, stay for a month and then go to Canada. This was not possible because we lost our visas for Canada in Kampala on our last day there and could not stay on because we would be captured by army soldiers if we did not leave in forty eight hours from receiving the visas to any country.

On July, 1972, my family and I had just moved from our block of flats to a new house in XXX. This house was situated on a hill. Fate was not good to us as we moved to our old block of flats and rented the new house to XXX for safety.

The block of flats consisted of XXX flats, and my father, together with another man, was the manager. Every night a member from each house went to a meeting, discussing the problems and helping each other. My friends and I used to have fun at night inside the building area for it was safely guarded by 'askaris' (guardsmen). We had many games like table tennis, badminton, marble gallery etc. We did not attend school for the last few months as girls were raped, if alone, by soldiers.

Thousands of people were slaughtered in secret at a place called 'Makindi'. The majority were Africans; educated ones. My father was taken four times to this place but luckily he had influence and got away at the cost of Shs. 40,000. An uncle of mine was taken away in the middle of the night. There is no trace of him till now.

When we went out shopping the soldiers would jeer at us and show us their guns. Housemaids and servants who cried at the departure of their employers were beaten up. Checkpoints were established at every ten kilometres. Many taxi-drivers were slashed. I have seen many killed. Others were just slumped in the boot of the car and taken to unknown torture places.

The worst thing was leaving my friends. Only a few were left when I left because most of them had left in early October. I can still picture the scene when all our employees were crying and my friends as well.

My uncle left in February, three months after the deadline, unable to go after what he had been through for example being stripped naked by the soldiers and being whipped. Many innocent citizens were shot; there were twelve public executions last summer. One of the men executed was known by my father, as a very honest, kind-hearted and non-political man.

> Although all this has happened in Uganda, I would someday like to return. Even if I do not get all that we owned back, I was born there and I would like to die there (Sikes, 1979, p. 133).

Seeking consent to publish was not an option because there was no name on the essay and nothing to identify which project school it had come from. However, my view was that the piece needed to be included in the book not least because it could remind teachers that they don't always know about what has happened in their students' lives and to alert them to the need to be sensitive when setting assignments, so I edited it to remove obvious identifiers. I reasoned that the events described were, unfortunately, not uniquely traceable to any one person and that the 6 years since they had occurred offered a further safeguard.

There was no reason to suspect that the piece was not an authentic record of a young girl's perceptions and experiences because it was written in a childish hand and, again, the account was similar to others that had come out of Uganda around the same time. In any case I took the line that literal truth was not essential here (Angrossino, 1998) and justified inclusion on the grounds that the piece did the work I wanted it to do. Of course, this all happened before the controversy over Rigoberta Menchu's autobiography erupted, at a time when I, and others, were perhaps not so sensitive to the sorts of truth issues such atrocity accounts could give rise to. Nowadays, maybe my thinking would have been slightly different and I may have introduced the piece with some sort of caveat to 'cover' both the claims I was re-presenting and to protect the author.

Impacting Lives and Manipulating Relationships

A few years on, working on a life history project investigating teachers' perceptions and experiences of teaching as a career (Sikes, Measor and Woods, 1985), I was made acutely conscious of how participating in narrative, auto/biographical research can impact on people's lives. This project involved teachers and researchers in a number of intensive interview conversations, in some cases spreading over 40 hours. Amongst the teachers I was working with was a man who wasn't happy in his job but who needed the salary it brought in to provide for his wife and four young children. The day he told me he was leaving teaching 'thanks to you because talking to you has made it clear to me that I need to get out even though I haven't as yet got anything to go to', made me realise the responsibility we take on when engaging in methods which have much in common with counselling approaches which have life change, rather than information collection, as a primary aim (see Bond, 2004; West and Byrne, 2009).

Then there was the unease I and my co-researcher, Linda Measor, began to feel as we reflected on how we could be seen to have manipulated relationships in order to get 'good' data (Measor and Sikes, 1992). Even though the project was focused on the development of professional lives, people told us about some very personal and intimate things (e.g. the death of a child; having an extra-marital affair; a criminal conviction) which they felt had influenced their careers. There was definitely a sort of confessional aspect to some of the interviews which may have had a cathartic effect for the teller but which equally definitely emphasised to us as researchers, our serious obligation to treat the accounts our particular methodological approach had elicited, in a respectful and careful manner. Having said that, it was hard (if not impossible) to discount what we knew when it came to analysis. Even though we did not breach confidences and spill beans what we were told inevitably shaped our understandings of influences on professional careers.

Ethics and Auto-Ethography

Particularly from the 1980s onwards, explicitly conscious narrative and auto/biographical turns can be tracked across a range of disciplines including anthropology, literary studies, historiography, philosophy, the humanities and law, as well as within the social sciences generally (see Bertaux, 1981 Chamberlayne, Bornat and Wengraf, 2000; Denzin and Lincoln, 2005; Hyvarinen, 2007; Plummer, 2000; Rorty, 1979). A proliferation of innovative methodologies and methods have accompanied, if not been a corollary, of this. Autoethnography (Ellis and Bochner, 2000; Ellis, 2004, 2009) is one such 'new' approach which has become especially popular.

I have long held the opinion that in investigating, analysing, making sense of and writing other people's lives, our own lives, our beliefs and values, our positionality, inevitably are implicated. In other words my view is that much, if not most, social science research is, to a degree at least, auto/biographical (Stanley, 1992, 1993: contributors to White Riley, 1988) and I had explicitly made reference to this belief in a book reporting a research project I undertook as a result of becoming a parent who was also a teacher (Sikes, 1997). Given this stance it is not surprising that when I first came across autoethnography, I found it very appealing. I was particularly attracted to it because I believed that this was an approach which offered a privileged opportunity to look at the meaning and experience of private 'troubles' in an evocative, narrative manner that would engage readers and which, possibly and if relevant, could lead to 'the indifference of publics being transformed into involvement with public issues' (Mills, 1970, p. 11–12). Even if 'troubles' were not the focus, autoethnography could prompt critical reflection on the personal experience of aspects of life as lived in particular social contexts, thereby broadening knowledge and understanding. The reflexive nature of the approach could also offer insights into the research process itself.

I understand that undertaking an autoethnography can be therapeutic for the researcher and that some advocates emphasise this value and the self knowledge benefits it can bring. My own preference though is for what has been described as analytic autoethnography (Anderson, 2006), in the tradition of autobiographical sociology (Merton, 1988). Expressing this preference is not to deny the personal value of therapeutic autoethnography or the benefits of giving voice and sharing experiences. Nor is it to say that emotional autoethnography cannot prompt transformational change (Ellis, Adams and Bochner, 2011). However, I do share William Housley and Robin Smith's (2011) view that autoethnographies which solely reify the academic self and personal experience and which sideline structures, systems 'organisational matters, framings and stratifications' can be analytically reductive (see also Delamont, 2007). And, as Yvonne Downs (in press and referencing Stanley and Wise, 1993) reminds us, as social scientists, that it is important not to confuse the personal with the confessional or revelatory. For my own part I have used narrative autoethnography on a number of occasions, in a number of ways and for a number of different reasons, including: to evoke a sense of feel and place (Sikes, 2005); to serve as a starting point for exploring shared experiences (Sikes, 1997, 2006b); as a basis for asking the sorts of troubling questions Mills suggests sociologists should be asking (Sikes, 2006b); as warning to other academics about how their work can be received quite differently to how they have intended (Sikes, 2008); and as a method of inquiry in working out a methodological position (Lavia and Sikes, 2010).

Despite my positive disposition towards the approach, as I have read more and more autoethnographic accounts I have came across work which has troubled me in different ways. In some cases the author's intention has been to unsettle and consequently they have revealed disturbing experiences in order to raise awareness, sensitise and potentially to incite action to bring about change. Carol Rambo Ronai's (1995) autoethnographic account of being a sexually abused child is an obvious example of this type of work. Other instances however, have perturbed because they have revealed exceptionally intimate, private and personal information about the author and also about people associated with them. It may seem to be citing the blindingly obvious but if an autoethnography is really by the person who is named as the author, whatever pseudonyms or fictional alterations and disguising strategies may be employed, everyone who appears in the narrative is identifiable, if not explicitly identified. This raises ethical questions (see Delamont, 2007; Tolich, 2010) about whether and to what extent permissions and consents have been obtained from people who by association appear in the narrative. There is also the issue of whether the author might come to regret their disclosure, although as both Carolyn Ellis (2009) and Carol Rambo (2007) point out, maybe it is up to autoethnographers themselves to take responsibility for their own writing, rather than for others to 'protect' them. My reading also suggests that some autoethnographies are what could be described as revenge texts with narratives of broken marriages and romantic relationships and stories of tensions and problems and cruelties within families or between friends/colleagues being not uncommon. 'Revenge which masquerades as sociological scholarship' (Sikes, 2010a, p. 16) or accounts which purport to be sociology yet have little or nothing to differentiate them from the misery memoirs which fill whole shelves of the book sections in many supermarkets are, I would argue, often both unethical and 'bad' sociology. The issue here, for me, circles around the notion of narrative power and questions about whose versions of truth are privileged. Tony Adams has written about these concerns and, furthermore, asks who has the ability to tell and who can listen to or, more pertinently have easy access to read, a particular story? He illustrates his discussion of these questions with his own writing about his relationship with his father, making the point that, as his dad is not an academic he is unlikely to read, or be able to respond in writing and in the same form, to what his son writes about him. This gives Adams some license to write about his parent in any way he likes without fear of contradiction or reprisal. However, this re-presentational freedom brings responsibility if he is to act ethically:

> I must understand, as best I can, how I may (re)present him, tempering any demonizing feelings I have while still allowing my story to unfold. My story will change knowing I have control over my father's portrayal, but being aware of this control is necessary when we write about others unable to tell their stories (Adams 2008, p. 181)

In these post-modern days most of us can cope with the notion of multiple realities and truths. We generally acknowledge too, that research narratives are not, nor ever can be, neutral straightforward recountings: even so, such understandings do not detract from the way in which published descriptions of people and events from lives take on a sort of 'reality' and a degree of fixity once out in the public domain. We know Adams senior via his son's account but we would have to hear what the father has to say if we are to get his perspective. When the people who are written about are not, for whatever reason, in a position to tell their story to the same audience, they are effectively silenced. From my own work (Sikes and Piper, 2010a) with teachers who were accused of sexual misconduct with pupils of which they said they were innocent, I am well aware that even when there is definitive and absolute proof of that innocence, the strength of 'no smoke without fire' thinking can mean that the accuser's story, as the first to be told, retains a power. The implications of this tendency for those identified or implicated in an autoethnographic narrative are clear.

At this point I would really like to have told a story which I don't feel ethically able to tell because it isn't mine alone (see Adams and Holman Jones, 2011, p. 109). The story that I can't tell is auto/biographical and it concerns particular troubling experiences around, and issues raised by, an autoethnographic doctoral thesis that I was one of the examiners of. Consequently, if I described specific and singular aspects of the case it would enable identification of all the other people who were involved or implicated. I could fictionalise the whole thing in an attempt at disguise (see Piper and Sikes, 2010; Sparkes, 1995, 2007), but even were I to do this, I doubt that I would be able to achieve what Martin Tolich (2004) calls 'internal confidentiality', where the 'internal' refers to the network of relationships which allow insiders to know and identify who and what is being described. Even were I to gain permission to offer my interpretations and understandings from all those who were immediately involved in the examination experience, there would still be those persons mentioned in the thesis who I could not contact and who were not, in any case, aware that they had been written about. Saying as much as I already have done could, in itself, be thought to give the game away to those in the know. However, since I have examined a number of doctorates that have taken an authoethnographic approach, and given that issues around research ethics, identification, confidentiality, truth and truths and treating people properly are pertinent to auto/biographical and narrative research and writing *per se*, I suspect that a number of people might read this and erroneously think that I am talking specifically about an instance known to them or even about themselves and their own work (see Mellick & Fleming, 2010, on such cases of mistaken identity). Once again I speak from experience because, in the past, when I have created composite fictional characters, readers have claimed to know exactly who I was writing about, and in all cases I had never even met the persons they named!

Although, the story I can't tell disturbed me on a number of fronts, here I am only going to talk about the issues it raised around seductive writing and identification of people described in autoethnographic and narrative research.

Seductive Writing

The best autoethnographies and narrative accounts are well written, are able to evoke an almost tangible sense of 'being there' and make readers want to read on to the end. An excellent example of what I mean is Carolyn Ellis' (2009) lyrical account of her childhood which, to me and to others I have discussed it with, evokes Norman Rockwell type pictures of rural American life in the 1950s. Although Virginia Woolf was talking specifically about fictional narrative when she wrote that

> the writer must get into touch with his *(sic)* reader by putting before him something which he recognises, which, therefore, stimulates his imagination, and makes him willing to co-operate in the far more difficult business of intimacy (1992: x).

What she says is of equal relevance to any genre of writing. Having said this, seductive writing, which elicits co-operation of the kind Woolf refers to can reel readers in ways which can cause them to feel uncomfortable or even tainted by giving them privileged knowledge of experiences, events, or feelings that they may believe are too intimate or personal or inappropriate or re-presented in too one-sided a fashion, to be shared. In some cases too, readers may find themselves in possession of information which makes them party to dangerous, potentially damaging or even possibly illegal activities which they may subsequently consider they have a responsibility to disclose to the appropriate authorities. Of course, it could be argued that people can always stop reading (although that privilege is not easily available to doctoral examiners), or that the work has done its intended job extremely well (as with the Rambo Ronai [1995] piece mentioned earlier). However here I come back to the concern that work which purports to be social science should do something more than lay bare personal troubles and preoccupations. It should too, be honest about exactly what it is, namely a personal, partisan re-presentation of events from the perspective of the author. Some authors argue that fictions can, in themselves, embody analysis and theory, making any explicatory work an unnecessary distraction which also takes away from the possibilities of the readers making their own interpretations. Andrew Sparkes, for instance, talks about 'active readership' (2003, p. 69) in which readers engage with a story, making their own sense by drawing on 'personal meanings gathered from outside the text' (*ibid*). However, even in his (2007) story

'*Embodiment, Academics and the Audit Culture*' which has (seduced and) resonated with academics worldwide (Sparkes, 2011), Sparkes makes clear what he is doing via an introduction and footnotes which explain where the story is rooted and how it articulates with previous scholarship. Thus he writes:

> here is a story that seeks to speak from the heart about the embodied struggles of a composite and mythical (perhaps?) academic at an imaginary (perhaps?) university in England that is permeated by an audit culture. It is based on informal interviews with academics at various universities in England and selected personal experiences. Thus, the constructive process is inspired by partial happenings, fragmented memories, echoes of conversations, whispers in corridors, fleeting glimpses of myriad reflections seen through broken glass, and multiple layers of fiction and narrative imaginings. In the end, the story simply asks for your consideration (Sparkes, 2007, p. 522).

In adding such an explication Sparkes acknowledges his position as an academic writer who bears both a responsibility to make interpretations and an obligation to take responsibility for those interpretations as conveyed through his storying. When Laurel Richardson notes, 'keeping the control of the text with its author... is especially important when one is writing personal narrative...It is the author's story, after all' (2007, p. 171) she is, I believe, asking for the ownership of writing to be acknowledged. This I believe to be particularly important if the author is especially skilled at crafting seductive stories.

Some Issues around Identification

These days informed consent is usually obtained from people who participate in research by completing questionnaires, by being interviewed or observed, by taking tests or by agreeing to join an experiment. In cases where, for whatever reason, the research participant is not able to make their own decision, a parent or guardian or someone with responsibility for their welfare, generally stands proxy for them. While some autoethnographers do seek consent from these they write about and/or may share their writing with those it concerns, allowing them to add their side of the story prior to publication, not all do. Consequently I have read autoethnographies which depict people other than the author in ways which could be personally, or even socially, damaging to them and to their family members, friends and colleagues. And once out there in the public domain, described and enshrined in print, people become fixed. Even if someone was once alcoholic for instance, it doesn't mean that five or ten years down the line they are still drinking. Yet if this is how they were depicted in a piece of autoethnographic writing which by its very nature identifies them, readers who are not aware of changed behaviours are likely to continue to believe that so and so's husband, father, mother, or whoever, is still a soak. Carrying such an identity can have serious and far reaching consequences which autoethnographers need to fully consider if their work is to be ethical and especially if they are intending to publish or in other ways put their writing out into the public domain under their own, rather than a pseudonymous, name.

I have written elsewhere (Sikes, 2010a) about the ways in which serendipity can intervene and stories can end up in unexpected places. Similarly, by the strange twists and turns that life takes, readers can find that they are reading about someone that they know. This can happen across continents and years and even accounts which authors believe are sufficiently distanced from those they describe may end up being read by a next door neighbour. Dame Pearlette Louisy has written about the problems of doing research in small island states and my St Lucian doctoral students, researching and writing about educational issues in a country whose population is around 165,000, know that they cannot realistically offer anonymity and definitely can't if there is any auto/biographical component to their work. In essence all auto/biographical writers have to be as similarly and acutely conscious of the potential impact of what they put into print. Kristina Medford's (2006) advice to researchers not to publish anything they wouldn't show to any one mentioned in the text is well worth bearing in mind.

FINALLY

Throughout this chapter a constant theme has been the importance and impact of historical and by implication, situational context when it comes to the consideration of ethical concerns (as of course, of everything else). By reflecting on over 30 years close acquaintanceship with, and involvement in, research and academic work which has had at least an autobiographical component, I have had the opportunity to trace changes in thinking and practice which, on the whole, have led to greater sensitivity and more ethical treatment of those whose lives are the focus of our social science activity. In 2003 Maggie MacLure noted that 'the pervasive concern in contemporary research' (2003, p.3) was avoiding the 'othering' of research participants. Undoubtedly how we engage people in research and how we re-present them has changed tremendously—and for the good - since when I started out. However, the current interest in explicitly personal writing coming at the same time as there would seem to be a global (or at least western) crisis of communal morality and ethics accompanied by a breakdown in trust, does bring its own dilemmas and issues which we do need to be mindful of. These dilemmas and issues would seem to warrant further and continuing examination and exploration leading, perhaps, to the development of a theory of context which could help to inform our narrative and autobiographical work and enable us to continue to advance practice in ethical directions.

Finally my litmus test, for whether or not I consider my own or other people's research and writing to be ethical is: how would I feel if I, members of my family, or my friends were to be involved and treated and written about in the way the research and writing in question involves or treats or depicts its participants? I also believe it to be important that writers explicitly take ownership of their words. For me, this means adopting high standards of authorial honesty. Earlier on I quoted Laurel Richardson's observation that 'narrativising, like all intentional behaviour.... is a site of moral responsibility' (1990, p. 131) and I return to those words here because, for me, they sum up the ethical imperative enjoined upon all researchers as they engage with and explore the relationships between epistemology, methodology, theory generation, re-presentation and truth. There is no doubt that researching, writing about and re-presenting lives carries a heavy ethical burden and we should always be mindful of that.

REFERENCES/BIBLIOGRAPHY

Adams, T. (2008). A review of narrative ethics. *Qualitative Inquiry, 14*(2), 175–194.

Adams, T., & Holman Jones, S. (2011). Telling stories: Reflexivity, queer theory and autoethnography. *Cultural Studies ⇔ Critical Methodologies, 11*(2), 108–116.

Allen, A., Anderson, K., Bristol, L., Downs, Y., O'Neill, D., Watts & Wu, Q. (2009). Resisting the unethical in formalised ethics: Perspectives and experiences. In J. Satterthwaite, H. Piper & P. Sikes (Eds.) *Power in the Academy*, 135–152. Stoke-on-Trent: Trentham Book.

Anderson, L. (2006). Analytic autoethnography. *Journal of Contemporary Ethnography 35*(4), 373–395.

Angrossino, M. (1998). *Opportunity house: Ethnographic studies of mental retardation.* Walnut Creek: AltaMira Press.

Appiah, K. (2010). *The honor code: How moral revolutions happen.* New York: W. W. Norton.

Attwood, M. (2008). Close to home: A celebration of Margaret Attwood. *Guardian Review,* 11 Oct: 2–4.

Bertaux, D. (1981). *Biography and society: The life history approach in the social sciences.* Beverley Hills, CA: Sage.

Boelen, W. A. M. (1992). Street corner society: Cornerville revisited. *Journal of Contemporary Ethnography, 21*(1), 11–51.

Bond, T. (2004). Ethical guidelines for researching counselling and psychotherapy. *Counselling and Psychotherapy Research, 4*(2), 10–19.

Bruner, J. (1993). The autobiographical process. In R. Folkenflik (Ed.) *The culture of autobiography: Constructions of self representation.* Stanford CA: Stanford University Press.

Cannella, G., & Lincoln, Y. (2007). Predatory vs dialogic ethics: Constructing an illusion or ethical practice as the core of research methods. *Qualitative Inquiry, 13*(3), 315–335.

Chamberlayne, P., Bornant, J., & Wengraf, T. (Eds.) (2000). *The turn to biographical methods in the social sciences: comparative issues and examples.* London, Routledge.

Delamont, S. (2007). Against autoethnography *http://www.cardiff.ac.uk/socsi/qualiti/Qualitative Researcher/QR_Issue4_Feb07.pdf* (accessed 10/4/11).

Denzin, N., & Lincoln, Y. (2005). Introduction: The discipline and practice of qualitative research. In N. Denzin and Y. Lincoln (Eds.) *The Sage handbook of qualitative research: Third edition,* 1–32. Thousand Oaks, Sage.

Downs, Y. (in press). Through the looking glass: Publishing in peer reviewed journals. *Power & Education.*

Ellis, C. (1986) *Fisher folk: Two communities on Chesapeake Bay.* Lexington: The University Press of Kentucky.

Ellis, C. (1995). Emotional and ethical quagmires in returning to the field. *Journal of Contemporary Ethnography,* 24, 68–98.

Ellis, C. (2004). *The ethnographic I: A methodological novel about autoethnography.* Walnut Creek, CA: AltaMira.

Ellis, C. (2007). Telling secrets, revealing lives: Relational ethics in research with intimate others. *Qualitative Inquiry, 13*(3), 3–29.

Ellis, C. (2009). *Revision: Autoethnographic reflections on life and work.* Walnut Creek: Left Coast Press.

Ellis, C., & Bochner, A. (2000). Autoethnography, personal narrative, reflexivity: researcher as subject. In N. Denzin & Y. Lincoln, (Eds.) *Handbook of Qualitative Ethnography: Second Edition.* Thousand Oaks: Sage: 733–768.
Ellis, C., Bochner, A., & Adams, T. (2010). Autoethnography: An overview. *FQS, 12*(1).
Fine, G. A. (1993). Ten lies of ethnography. *Journal of Contemporary Ethnograph, 22*(3), 267–294.
Flyvbjerg, B. (2001). *Making social science matter: Why social inquiry fails and how it can succeed again.* Cambridge: Cambridge University Press.
Goodson, I., & Sikes, P. (2001). *Life history in educational settings: Learning from lives.* Buckingham: Open University Press.
Haggarty, K. D. (2004). Ethics creep: Governing social science research in the name of ethics. *Qualitative Sociology, 27*(4), 391–414.
Halse, C., & Honey, A. (2007). Rethinking ethics review as institutional discourse. *Qualitative Inquiry, 13*(3), 336–352.
Hammersley, M. (2009). Against the ethicists: On the evils of ethical regulation. *International Journal of Social Research Methodology, 12*(3), 217–218.
Housley, W., & Smith, R. (2011). Innovation and reduction in contemporary qualitative methods: The case of conceptual coupling, activity-type pairs and auto-ethnography sociological research. Online, *15*(4), p. 9, <http://www.socresonline.org.uk/15/4/9.html> 10.5153/sro.2216
Hyvarinen, M. (2007). 'Revisiting the narrative turns', paper presented at ESRC Seminar *'Narrative Turn: Revisioning Theory'*, University of Edinburgh, 23/3/08.
Israel, M., & Hay, I. (2006). *Research ethics for social scientists.* London: Sage.
Lavia, J., & Sikes, P. (2010). 'What part of me do I leave out?' In pursuit of decolonising practice. *Power & Education, 2*(1). http://www.wwwords.co.uk/pdf/validate.asp?j=power&vol=2&issue=1&year=2010&article=7_Lavia_POWER_2_1_web
Lincoln, Y. (2005). Institutional review boards and methodological conservatism: The challenge to and from phenomenological paradigms. In N. Denzin & Y. Lincoln (Eds.) *The Sage Handbook of Qualitative Research: Third Edition,* 165–181. Thousand Oaks: Sage.
Lincoln, Y., & Denzin, N. (2005). Epilogue: The eighth and ninth moments—Qualitative research in/and the fractured future. In N. Denzin & Y. Lincoln (Eds.) *The Sage Handbook of Qualitative Research: Third Edition,* 1115–1126. Thousand Oaks: Sage.
Lincoln, Y., & Cannella, G. (2009). Ethics and the broader rethinking/reconceptualization of research as construct. *Cultural Studies ⇔ Critical Methodologies 9*(2), 273–285.
Macfarlane, B. (2009). *Researching with integrity: The ethics of academic research.* London: Routledge.
MacLure, M. (2003). *Discourse in educational and social research.* Buckingham: Open University.
Measor, L. & Sikes, P. (1992). Visiting lives: Ethics and methodology in life history. In I. Goodson (Ed.) *Studying Teachers' Lives,* 209–233. London, Routledge.
Medford, K. (2006). Caught with a fake ID: Ethical questions about slippage in autoethnography. *Qualitative Inquiry, 12*(5), 835–864.
Mellick, M., & Fleming, S. (2010). Personal narrative and the ethics of disclosure: A case study from elite sport. *Qualitative Research, 10*(3), 299–314.
Mills, C. W. (1970). *The sociological imagination.* Harmondsworth: Penguin (first published in 1959 by Oxford University Press).
Moen, T. (2006). Reflections on the narrative research approach. In *International Journal of Qualitative Methods,* 5(4), 56–69.
Pelias, R. (2004). *A Methodology of the heart,* Walnut Creek: AltaMira.
Plummer, K. (2000) *Documents of Life 2: An Invitation to a Critical Humanism* London, Sage
Piper, H., & Sikes, P. (2010). 'All teachers are vulnerable, but especially gay teachers': Using composite fictions to protect research participants in pupil-teacher sex related research. *Qualitative Inquiry 16*(7), 566–574.
Pring, R. (2000). *Philosophy of educational research.* London: Continuum.

Rambo Ronai, C. (1995). Multiple reflections of child sex abuse: An argument for a layered account. *Journal of Contemporary Ethnography*, 23, 395–426.

Rambo, C. (2007). Handing IRB an unloaded gun. *Qualitative Inquiry, 13*(3), 353–367.

Rorty, R. (1979). *Philosophy and the mirror of nature*. Princeton, NJ: Princeton University Press.

Richardson, L. (1990). Narrative and sociology. *Journal of Contemporary Ethnography, 19*(1), 116–135.

Richardson, L. (1994). Research: A method of inquiry. In N. Denzin & Y. Lincoln (Eds.) *Handbook of Qualitative Research*, 516–629. Walnut Creek: Sage.

Richardson, L. (2000). Writing: A method of inquiry. In N. Denzin & Y. Lincoln (Eds.) *The Handbook of Qualitative Research* (2nd ed.), 923–948. Thousand Oaks: Sage.

Richardson, L. (2007). *Last writes: A daybook for a dying friend*. Walnut Creek, CA: Left Coast Press.

Sikes, P. (1979). (reprinted 1984). *Teaching about race relations*. Norwich: CARE U.E.A

Sikes, P. (1986). *The mid-career teacher: Adaptation and motivation in a contracting secondary school system*. University of Leeds. Unpublished Ph.D. Thesis.

Sikes, P. (1997). *Parents who teach: Stories from home and from school*. London: Cassells.

Sikes, P. (2000). 'Truth' and 'lies' revisited. *British Educational Research Journal, 26*(2), 257–269.

Sikes, P. (2005). Storying schools: Issues around attempts to create a sense of feel and place in narrative research writing. *Qualitative Research, 5*(1), 79–94.

Sikes, P. (2006a) On dodgy ground? Problematics and ethics in educational research? *International Journal of Research & Method in Education, 29*(1), 105–117.

Sikes, P. (2006b). Making the strange familiar *OR* travel broadens the mind: A story of a visiting academic. *Qualitative Inquiry, 12*(3), 523–540.

Sikes, P. (2006c). 'Scandalous Stories and dangerous liaisons: When male teachers and female pupils fall in love. *Sex Education, 6*(3), 265–280.

Sikes, P. (2008). At the eye of the storm: An academic(s) experience of moral panic. *Qualitative Inquiry 14*(2), 235–25.

Sikes, P. (2009). The study of teachers' lives and careers: An auto/biographical life history of the genre. In J. Satterthwaite, H. Piper, & P. Sikes (Eds.) *Power in the Academy*. Stoke-On-Trent: Trentham Books.

Sikes, P. (2010a). The ethics of writing life histories and narratives in educational research. In A. Bathmaker & P. Harnett (Eds.) *Exploring learning, identity and power through life history and narrative research*. London: Routledge/Falmer.

Sikes, P. (2010b). Researching teacher-student sexual relations: Key risks and ethical issues. *Ethnography and Education, 5*(2), 143–157.

Sikes, P., & Goodson, I. (2003). Living research: Thoughts on educational research as moral practice. In P. Sikes, J. Nixon, & W. Carr, (Eds.) *The moral foundations of educational research: Knowledge, inquiry and values*, 32–51. Maidenhead: Open University Press/McGraw Hill Educational.

Sikes, P., Measor, L., & Woods, P. (1985). *Teacher careers: Crises and continuities:* Lewes: Falmer Press.

Sikes, P., & Piper, H. (2010a). *Researching sex and lies in the classroom: Allegations of sexual misconduct in schools*. London: Routledge/Falmer Press.

Sikes, P. & Piper, H. (2010b). Ethical research, academic freedom and the role of ethics committees and review procedures in education. *International Journal of Research and Method in Education, 33*(3), 205–213.

Sikes, P., & Piper, H. (Eds.) (2011). *Ethics and Academic freedom in educational research*. London: Routledge.

Sparkes, A. (1995). Physical education teachers and the search for self: Two cases of structured denial. In N. Armstrong (Ed.) *New Directions in Physical Education*, 3, 157–178. London: Cassell.

Sparkes, A. (2003). Men, sport, spinal cord injury and narrative time. *Qualitative Research, 3*(3) 295–320

Sparkes, A. (2007). Embodiment, academics and the audit culture. *Qualitative Research, 7*(4), 521–550.

Sparkes, A. (2011). The power of stories: The audit culture—laughing, crying and surviving. Keynote presentation at the discourse, power, resistance conference. University of Plymouth, 14/4/11.

Stanley, E. (1992). *The auto/biographical I: theory and practice of feminist auto/biography.* Manchester: Manchester University Press.

Stanley, E. (1993). On auto/biography in sociology. *Sociology, 27*(1), 41–52.

Stanley, L., & Wise, E. (1993). B*reaking out again: feminist ontology and epistemology.* London: Routledge.

Stenhouse, L., Verma, G., Wild, R., & Nixon, J. (1982). *The problems and effects of teaching about race relations.* London: Routledge.

Thomas, W. I. & Znaniecki, F. (1918–1920). *The polish peasant in Europe and America* (2nd ed.). Chicago: University of Chicago Press.

Tierney, W. & Blumberg Corwin, Z. (2007). The tensions between academic freedom and institutional review boards. *Qualitative Inquiry, 13*(3), 388–398.

Tolich, M. (2004). Internal confidentiality: When confidentiality assurances fail relational informants. *Qualitative Sociology, 27*(1), 101–106.

Tolich, M. (2010). A critiques of current practice: Ten foundational guidelines for autoethnographers. *Qualitative Health Research, 20*(12), 1599–1610.

Tullis Owen, J., McRae, C., Adams, T., & Vitale, A. (2009). Truth troubles. *Qualitative Inquiry 15*(1), 178–200.

West, W., & Byrne, J. (2009). Some ethical concerns about counselling research. *Counselling Psychology Quarterly, 22*(3), 309–319.

White Riley, M. (Ed.) (1988). *Social change and the life course: Volume 2 – Sociological Lives.* Thousand Oaks: Sage.

Whyte, W. F. (1943). *Street corner society: the social structure of an Italian slum.* Chicago: University of Chicago Press.

Whyte, W. F. (1992). In defence of street corner society. *Journal of Contemporary Ethnography, 21*(1), 52–68.

Woolf, V. (1992). Mr Bennett and Mrs Brown. In V. Woolf & R. Bowlby (eds.) *A woman's essays.* London: Penguin.

AFFILIATION

Pat Sikes
University of Sheffield

MARIE KARLSSON AND HÉCTOR PÉREZ PRIETO

12. PROFESSIONAL IDENTITIES IN RETIRED TEACHER EDUCATORS' LIFE STORIES

The Global and Local Contexts of Life Story Interviews

The general aim of this chapter is to contribute to the relatively under-researched area of the working lives and professional identities of teacher educators in Sweden and elsewhere by discussing the functions that generate identity in the design and execution of life story research in particular.

The professional identities of teacher educators have up until recently received little attention from researchers. According to Murray and Harrison (2008), the 80s and 90s saw little research on this occupational group and, although the situation has improved, it is still an under-researched area (see also Zeichner, 1999; Swennen and Bates, 2010). In the research that has been done with this focus, teacher educators stand out as a motley crew, coming from different directions with different experiences and competencies and with different educational tasks to perform. This is vividly pictured in Cochran-Smith's (2003, p. 22) description of teacher educators in the USA as members of part-time or temporary adjunct faculty, fieldwork supervisors, graduate students, school-based personnel, coordinators and professors. Another important issue here is that teaching teacher education is a second career for many people (Acker, 1997).

Since the Swedish teacher education was incorporated into the university in 1977, it has grown considerably and been the object of several political reforms. Today, it is undergoing yet another reform and at the same time a large group of teacher educators born in the 1940s are reaching retirement. Many of these retiring teacher educators have been working with teacher education for decades and have experienced several educational reforms and societal changes restructuring teacher education in Sweden. If we want to gain an understanding of teacher education, it is essential to learn about the working lives and professional identities of teacher educators. And if we want to learn about the working lives and professional identities of teacher educators, the best way to do this is to ask them to tell stories about their professional lives.

Research explicitly focusing on the professional identities of teacher educators is still quite hard to find, although some can be found in the growing literature on the professional development of teacher educators (Swennen and Bates, 2010). One such example is Lunenberg and Hamilton (2008), who discuss teacher educator identities in relation to the national contexts of teacher education in the Netherlands and the USA and point to the plurality within and between the two systems of teacher education. According to Lunenberg and Hamilton, the multiple

Ivor F. Goodson, Avril M. Loveless and David Stephens (Eds.), Explorations in Narrative Research, 141–152.
© 2012 Sense Publishers. All rights reserved.

career paths leading into teacher education and the lack of institutionalised preparation for the job contribute to the vagueness regarding the identities of teacher educators, an indefiniteness that makes teacher educators' personal histories affect the profession more significantly than is the case with other professions. They argue further that 'the profession of teacher educator is neither well-defined nor recognised as being an important profession on its own merits and this seems to have effects on the identity of teacher educators' (p. 186). Since a great deal of research on teacher educators' professional lives and identities is conducted by teacher educators through self-study, the research can in itself be seen as an ongoing struggle for professionalization.

Research on teacher educators in Sweden has to a large extent been dominated by a focus on questions concerning the relations between theory and practice, in which teacher educators have been viewed as either agents of or resistance to change in processes of policy implementation (Askling, 1983; Carlgren, 1992; Beach, 1995, Erixon Arreman, 2005). A great deal of Swedish research on teacher educators has thus been conducted within areas involving recurrent political reforms. As we are interested in learning about the long-term development and changes affecting the working lives and identities of this occupational group in Sweden, we have chosen to study the life stories of recently retired teacher educators with experience from working with teacher education for more than twenty years at our own department. This group of informants was chosen because, for many people, retirement is a time of change that is well suited to reflection on past experiences and planning for a new life. Moreover, the life stories of teacher educators with long working experiences can make visible the impact earlier teacher education reforms has had through the ways individual educators make sense of having had to deal with restructuring and changes. Along with Lunenberg and Hamilton (2008), we argue that we can learn a great deal of the professional identities of teacher educators by listening to their work life stories.

LIFE STORY AND IDENTITY

The concept of identity needs to be addressed explicitly in any discussion of life story telling as identity making. A conceptualisation of identity as a combination of ongoing social processes of identification rather than a step-by-step development of individual characteristics is widely recognised in contemporary theory (Jenkins 2008; Gee 2001). Discussing the concepts of self and identity in research on teacher education, Rodgers and Scott (2008, p. 733) point to contemporary conceptions of identity as formed through relationships—multiple, unstable and shifting; contextually situated—and as involving the construction and reconstruction of storied meaning. According to the perspective on identity presented by Jenkins (2008, p. 17), the social act of identifying oneself or others as someone or something has to do with meaning, interaction, agreement, disagreement, convention, innovation, communication and negotiation. The epistemological stance we take from this perspective on identity is social constructionist for the reason that the personal and professional identities of individuals are understood as maintained, managed, and re-negotiated in relation to other individuals and groups and to available institutional and societal discourse. In this view, the study of the professional identities of teacher educators can benefit from studies of life stories as ongoing social processes of identification and sense making.

The biographical interview or life story interview has not gained much attention as a social practice shaping and being shaped by the stories told within it. This has been pointed out in an eloquent way by Mishler (1999) and more recently by Helsig (2010). Although there seems to be a tacit agreement among life story researchers that narrative identities are social identities, the social dimensions of life story interviews are more or less neglected in favour of story content. A recent debate in narrative research has raised this question of the interview as interactional context for the study of selfhood and identity. The debate concerns the pros and cons of, on the one hand, reflective narratives told in interview settings (big stories) and on the other, stories told in the immediate interactions of everyday life (small stories), (Bamberg, 2006; Freeman, 2006). According to Freeman (2006, p. 132), who has participated in the debate as a kind of advocate of a big story-approach, small stories are 'closer to the action and enmeshed within the interactive, especially conversational, dynamics of social life while big ones are more removed and tend to efface the social dimension'. In the study of narrative identity small story-research places emphasis on how selves and identities are accomplished *in interaction* through the use of stories, while big story-research emphasises the identities shaped in *stories about* past interactions and events. The differences between these approaches can be said to be somewhat exaggerated and many life story researchers can be said to have a foot in both camps (Mishler, 1999; Goodson, et. al., 2010). Following De Fina (2009), we argue that the context of the life story interview should be treated as one of many possible interactional contexts and analysed as shaping and being shaped by the interlocutors' storytelling (see also Karlsson, 2006).

However, what seems to be missing in this debate is reflection on the context of the design and execution of the research project through which different forms of stories and storytelling are studied. Whether the selection and production of data are done through audio- or video-recordings of storytelling in everyday conversations or life story interviews, the design of the study conditions and becomes a part of the participants' storytelling as much as any immediate interactional context. This is dealt with by Lucius-Hoene and Deppermann (2000), who point out that the interviewer and interviewee have made assumptions about the purpose of the research and about each other long before the actual interview conversation takes place, assumptions that shape and are shaped by the future interview conversation. They have developed a model of the biographic interviewing process that consists of three frames: 1. The pre-communicative situation in which the researcher formulates research topics, methodology and criteria for recruitment of participants; 2. First contact between researcher and participants during the recruitment process when the setting and topics for the interviews are presented to the interviewees; and 3. The actual interview encounter.

In an attempt to answer the question if and how methodological tools of small story-approaches could be productively integrated into big story research, Helsig (2010) has renamed the first and second frame in Lucius-Hoene and Deppermann's model the global interview context, and the third frame the local interview context.

This chapter will discuss how the recruitment of research participants and the relations between the interviewer and interviewee in the global interview context can be seen as partly shaping the stories told in the local interview context. The point here is that when we as researchers approach people to engage them in our research on life stories, we identify them and they identify us as certain kinds of people. It would obviously be more or less impossible to conduct research if we did not identify the people whose life stories we want to research, but it is still interesting to discuss in what ways the identification of research participants in the global interview context becomes part of the stories told in the interview encounters. Is there a risk that we interpret the life stories of research participants as meaningful only in relation to the social identities we as researchers have placed them in to fit the aims and design of our projects? This is an even more delicate question for researchers who claim to be interested in peoples' actions, experiences and reflections about their lives.

In the following presentation and discussion of the work life stories of two experienced teacher educators, the claims of professional identity made in the stories will be analysed as partly conditioned by the recruitment-process and by the relations between interviewers and the interviewees as employees at the same department.

Project, Method and Data

The life story data presented in this chapter are drawn from an ongoing study on the life stories of experienced teacher educators named, 'Retired Teacher Educators' Storied Experiences from Teacher Education' (Pérez Prieto, 2008). An important background for the project is the recurrent and far-reaching reforms of the Swedish teacher education since its incorporation into the university in 1977. These three decades have seen a major quantitative expansion of teacher education, great efforts to integrate teacher education programmes into the academia, and previously differentiated teacher education programmes have been integrated and are now being re-formed into separate programmes again as part of the latest reform (Gov. Bill 2009/10:89). The integration of different teacher education programmes was initiated during the 1970s and consolidated through the 2001 reform when all teacher students entered the same teacher education programme together (students wanting to become preschool teachers took courses together with students aiming to teach in upper secondary school) and later choose their specialisations. The ideology of integration benefitted some and marginalised others as will be shown in our discussion of the two working life stories. The latest reform has moved the Swedish teacher education in the opposite direction as it promotes segregation and explicit demarcations between the different teacher education programmes. A large group of teacher educators has spent a big part of their working lives as participants in the making and re-making of teacher education since the 70s. Many of these experienced teacher educators are now reaching retirement age or have already retired. The overall aim of the project is to learn about this rich period of Swedish teacher education through their life stories.

The focus of attention in this chapter is the life stories and narrative identities of two recently retired teacher educators, here called Siw and Kjell, who have worked at the same department as us. At the time when the aim of the project was formulated, Kjell had already retired and Siw was going to retire in less than a year. By that time Héctor had worked at the university for five years while Marie was newly employed as a junior research fellow. As the recruitment process is considered part of the data in this chapter, it will be presented in more detail in the next section. Siw has been interviewed three times by Marie, the first two times at Siw's office at the department and the last interview took place in her home. Kjell has been interviewed by Héctor three times, twice in Héctor's office at the department and once in Kjell's home. Héctor's interviews with Kjell and Marie's first two interviews with Siw were conducted during the spring of 2008. The third and last of Marie's interviews with Siw was conducted three years later in the spring of 2011. The interviews were conducted as traditional life story interviews, one and a half up to two hour conversations guided by the interviewers' interest in the lives and personal experiences of the interviewees within the areas of education, working life and teacher education.

As we view the life story interviews as social processes of identification, we draw on a model for positioning analysis of narrative interaction developed by Bamberg (1997). This model takes the interview context into consideration when looking at how different identity positions are invoked, rejected or re-negotiated in the recounted work life stories and through the telling of the stories in the immediate interview conversation (see also Karlsson and Evaldsson, 2011). A third level of this model, not dealt with in this chapter, considers how these positions invoke or resist dominant discourse. Instead of copying Bamberg's model, we introduce a fourth level of positioning analysis. Following Helsig (2010), we include positionings made in the global interview context. This makes the pre-interview relations between interviewers and interviewees, including the recruitment processes, part of the working life stories and relevant to the analysis of storied identities.

In the following section we will point out how identity claims made in life story interviews can be seen as shaped by and re-shaping the very aim and design of the research project and by previous relations between interviewer and interviewee. We both will make the presentations of the stories and narrative identities taking shape in the global and local interview contexts as first person accounts.

Siw —I am no teacher educator

The first time I (Marie) spoke to Siw about her participation in the project at the beginning of the year 2008 she bluntly asked me what I was after. I remember feeling awkward under her suspicious gaze when I started to explain that it was *her experiences* of working as a teacher educator that I was interested in and not something I had figured out in advance. The thing was that Siw had been asked, by another project co-worker, to participate in the study before I spoke to her, and thus had had some time to think about it. Obviously she had her doubts about the study, the researchers involved and her participation in it. This encounter was also the first time we spoke to each other. I had just begun working at the department and Siw usually spent her coffee and lunch breaks in one of the two lunch rooms where I almost never went. Three years and three interview conversations have passed since this meeting, and I can still remember the feeling of being thrown off balance by her direct question. I can also see our encounter as part of Siw's stories about her working life, in which images of narrow-minded and short-sighted researchers and professors frequently feature. What I did not know then, and what will be the focus of this section of the chapter, is that Siw never wanted to see herself as an educator of teachers but of leisure-time pedagogues.

During the two first interviews with Siw the conversation shifted between her early experiences of education and working life and the gradual down-sizing of the leisure-time pedagogue education programme at Karlstad University.

Leisure-time Pedagogues are not Teachers

Siw started working at the teacher seminar as a lecturer in leisure-time activity in 1977, the year of the university reform, as a teacher of leisure-time pedagogues (*fritidspedagoger*). She took part in building this educational programme from scratch. From what I know now, it is fair to say that the aim of our project and my answer to her question, 'it's your experiences of working as a teacher educator that I'm interested in', put her in a bad position. The suspiciousness I had sensed in Siw at our first encounter also showed in the beginning of our first interview. Just after I had turned on the digital Dictaphone she turned quiet while I blabbered on about my experiences of interviewing and about the effect audio-recording devices had on some interview conversations. When I turned silent as well she said; 'Yea, I'm not sure about what you want to know' (beginning of 1st interview).

As I had done when we first met, I started to explain the aim of the project and how we, me and Héctor, saw the experiences of teacher educators like herself and others as offering valuable insights into the history of the growth and changes of the local teacher education. After having listened to me she expressed doubts about remembering anything. Maybe she experienced the interview situation as some kind of test. While I assured her that I did not expect her to deliver a rehearsed story about her life, she told me that she had been in a second-hand store and found a copy of two old school calendars from the local teacher education, the academic years of 1976/77 and 77/78. She showed me the 76/77 calendar, and I remember wondering if she had prepared for the interview by bringing it. The calendar had pictures of every student in every class, and Siw showed it to me as an example of what was a good system. 'You can see that we had a **great** system with **pictures** of all the students in the different classes…you don't have that today' (Beginning of 1st interview). Nowadays, Siw said, you have to photograph the students yourself.

She continued to tell me that the calendar was a good source of information as it had the names of all the department heads and board members listed. Then she showed me that she was listed as chair of the board for the leisure-time pedagogue education programme. There was also a board for the preschool teacher education programme and one for the teacher education programmes as well.

This way, Siw positioned herself as an educator of leisure-time pedagogues and not a teacher educator. After this clarifying start of our first interview, Siw told me about her personal history, education and work experiences before she started working in Karlstad. After about an hour of talk about her early work life experiences she returned to the time, in the late seventies, when the leisure-time pedagogue education program was truly separate from the programmes educating preschool teachers and teachers. She worked together with a colleague and followed classes of students throughout their whole education.

> We didn't have anything to do with the teacher education program... and we didn't have anything to do with the preschool teachers either [M: That was just the way it was?] that's the way it was. They are two separate professions. Some say leisure-time pedagogues and preschool teachers work in similar ways, but they don't. Maybe it's because preschool teachers worked with the education of leisure-time pedagogues **until** there were educated leisure-time pedagogues who could take over (From the 1st interview).

Siw claims an identity as one of these educated leisure-time pedagogues who took over. As time went by she watched the unique character of the education program lose its distinct profile and the professional identity of leisure-time pedagogues weaken. Since the reform of 2001, all teacher education programs were partly integrated and all students took the same courses in the early stages of the training regardless of whether they were studying to become preschool teachers or leisure-time pedagogues. This is something Siw returns to in all three interviews.

> Today the profession is ruined. Leisure-time pedagogues are expected only to work in schools and students only do their in-service training in schools [M: Why has it turned out this way?] Don't ask me why. I think it's because those who have designed the education program don't know what it means to be a leisure-time pedagogue (From the 2nd interview).

She partly blames the university for this and states that efforts to raise the status of an education program must begin with the mentioning of its name.

If you turn to psychology, you know that a child who is never called by its name loses its identity...what about a profession that is never mentioned by its name. And here we have highly educated professors, pedagogues and researchers and god knows what. They should know this.

The unique character and gradual decline of the leisure-time pedagogue education program is a recurrent theme in Siw's stories. It can even be seen as a story in itself and as a backdrop to many of her work life stories. This makes our pre-interview encounter stand out as confirmation of her repeatedly claimed position as a non-teacher educator. Siw got the attention of researchers for being in a place where she didn't want to be, teaching student teachers.

Kjell – we worked together

I (Héctor) first met Kjell when I started working at the University as a senior lecturer seven years ago in 2004. At that time Kjell had a couple of years left before retirement and was among other things in charge of teacher education internationalisation projects at the department. This led to us to taking a joint trip to Chile, my native country, where we visited several different teacher education institutions trying to initiate cooperation projects. While we were there, we also took the opportunity to meet with relatives of mine. We also talked about my experiences of attending teacher training in Chile during the social and political upheavals surrounding the 1973 revolution.

A couple of years later I called Kjell at home and told him about the project and asked him if he wanted to participate, which he did. He did not ask any questions about the project, not on the phone, or when we met in my office for the first interview. When I think about why he chose to participate, my guess is that our shared experiences had given him some confidence in me as researcher and that he saw research in general as a good thing. When we sat down to talk about Kjell's experiences of his life as a teacher educator, our shared travelling experiences in Chile most certainly contributed to making the interview conversations free and easy-going.

Reminiscing About the Good Old Days

Kjell started working at the teacher seminar in 1970 as a teacher in education. At the end of the second interview, conducted in Kjell's study at home, he started talking about his work during the seventies. When I listened to the recording some time later, I noticed that the stories he told changed character as he started to use the pronoun 'we' much more frequently than he had before. Up until a point, Kjell had told stories about his life from the perspective of an individual self, 'my childhood in the north of Värmland'. Then Kjell suddenly starts to tell stories about his work as a teacher educator in which he positions himself as part of a collective of teacher educators working together with the student collective towards the common goal of bringing about changes in the content and organisation of teacher education.

> After 1968–69 the student teachers demanded to be included in the organisation of teacher education. These years saw some very radical student teachers. They arranged meetings and were very politically active at the beginning of the 70s, you could say during all of the 70s until the beginning of the 80s. This ended when we got the new right-wing government in the early 80s. There wasn't much enthusiasm left by that time. But the 70s was a very interesting period when it came to methods of teaching. We teacher educators worked **hard** to change the prevalent methods of teaching at the

old teacher training college. We started to cooperate much more between the programmes (From the 2nd interview).

But there was external pressure for change as well, Kjell said just as we were about to end our second interview. He mentions the reports (SOU 1972, p. 26 and 27) that came to play an important part in the upcoming reformation of teacher education. According to Kjell, the commission emphasised cooperation instead of authority, and this was something new. 'Something I hadn't experienced before and never have since then... that you took a stand, ideologically' (from the 2nd interview).

A few weeks later, I met Kjell once again for a third interview in my office at the university. I started the conversation by asking him to tell me more about the ideological impact of the commission and about the changes the teacher educators and students worked to achieve. Kjell once again talks about the time after the years of 68–69 as a time of ideology and change in teacher education, among students and teachers. The positioning of teacher educators as a collective working to reach the same goals is made in greater detail than in the second interview.

> Together with the students we tried to change the teaching practices. I remember in 1975 we had a joint project where teacher educator and student teachers from different programs worked together... We always tried to integrate groups of student teachers from different programs. Since then and up until I retired, this idea has permeated the teacher education in Karlstad... we worked for a perspective on education, teaching and children as parts of a whole. We wanted all categories of teachers to learn about all stages of children's schooling, from the youngest to the oldest children.

Kjell's stories about his experiences of working as a teacher educator in the 70s are characterised by repeated positionings of teacher educators and student teachers as collectives, taking ideological stands and sharing common goals. This mode of storytelling can be understood as partly shaped by our respective experiences of being young in the 70s and partly by the revolutionary times as teacher and student in different national contexts. The pre-interview relation between me and Kjell was partly shaped during our joint trip to Chile, where we also had time to talk and share experiences. This shared frame of reference surely facilitates this joint reminiscing about the good old days in the 70s. The stories of the 'good old days' also function as a reaction against an upcoming teacher education reform aiming to reinstall the system of separate teacher education programs that were integrated through the last reform in 2001.

Discussion

In line with the two aims of this chapter, an interesting aspect of the different, even diverging, positionings of professional identities discussed here is that they tell us something important about how the narrative positionings of professional identities of teacher educators are closely intertwined with both the policy context and the social encounters in global interview contexts. In Siw's stories, the integration of teacher education programs of the 2001 reform, that Kjell told stories about fighting for, led to a decline of the unique character of the leisure-time pedagogue education program and thus of Siw's professional identity as an educator of leisure-time pedagogues. Kjell, who only once briefly mentioned the leisure-time pedagogue program, told stories of how his dreams from the 70s were slowly realised and finally officially implemented with the 2001 reform. This analysis makes visible how what Mills (1959, p. 226) calls 'the human meaning of public issues' can be understood when related to problems or troubles in the lives of individuals. And as the latest teacher education reform re-installs the system with separate programs we can say that Siw's story is the one with the happy ending, while Kjell's retirement has saved him from the experience of a complete reversion to what he spent a large part of his working life fighting to achieve. The professional identity claims made by the participating teacher educators reveal power struggles between different categories of teacher educators as a fundamental ingredient in the working lives of this occupational group (see also Beach, 1995; Carlgren, 1992). Perhaps there is a need to question the supposed neutrality of the occupational title 'teacher educator' as it blends the different colours of this motley crew together. Or, maybe another way forward (or sideways) is to follow the notion of identity as a social process of identification towards an understanding of professional identity as a constant becoming instead of a striving towards a goal of fixed identities and belongings. When asked to tell our life story, we are offered the opportunity of *becoming* someone in the eyes of the other person. Siw and Kjell told us stories of their working life experiences that made visible their pursuit of *becoming* professional educators within their fields of expertise. At the same time, in the very act of *telling* their life stories, they expressed their will to become a certain kind of educators in our eyes as interviewers, researchers and colleagues. As researchers of life stories and identities we are part of these processes of identification as soon as we start to formulate research questions and project designs.

Furthermore, regardless of how openly we as researchers approach the people whose life stories we wish to learn about, we still identify them as certain kinds of people belonging to this or that social group. In a sense, we approach people with our wishes and expectations in ways that condition the stories they tell. Conceptualising identity as social processes of identification (Jenkins 2008; Gee 2001) can contribute to the field of research on life story and identity as it allows for an understanding of the ways in which the research community takes part in the ongoing co-construction of professional identities.

As we see it, the challenge here is to listen to people's stories closely and let them be heard above or in chorus with the voices of our own research agendas. The life story interview also makes it possible for research participants like Siw to resist or re-negotiate the identities imposed on them by researchers in a way that is less open to people engaged in non-participatory research. There are many ways of looking beyond the local context of the life story interview to understand the stories told within it. A nowadays well-treaded path for life story researchers is to situate the stories told in social and political contexts in order to facilitate broader understandings of teachers' work and lives. In other words, the researchers contextualise the life story, thus turning it into life history. This has been pointed out and discussed by, for example, Goodson (1997) and Goodson and Sikes (2001), who have also issued warnings against an unreflective celebration of teachers' personal stories that ignore social contexts. We embrace that approach while wishing to suggest that the local and global interview context of the actual *telling* of life stories should be included in the analysis as elements shaping the stories told and the identities they invoke and resist. The occupational title 'teacher educator' turned out to be both emotionally charged and neutral in ways that we as researchers had not imagined as we set out to do this study. This 'discovery' emphasises one of the strengths of the life story approach, namely its potential to accommodate the unexpected.

REFERENCES

Acker, S. (1997). Becoming a teacher educator: Voices of woman academics in Canadian faculties of education. *Teaching and Teacher Education 13*(1), 6–74.

Askling, B. (1983). *Utbildningsplanering i en lärarutbildning. En studie av läroplansarbete i den decentraliserade högskolan* (Studies in Education and Psychology 12). Stockholm: CWK Gleerup.

Bamberg, M. (1997). Positioning between structure and performance. *Journal of Narrative and Life History, 7*, 335–342.

Bamberg, M. (2006). Stories: Big or small: Why do we care? *Narrative Inquiry, 16*(1), 139–147.

Beach, D. (1995). *Making sense of the problems of change: An ethnographic study of a teacher education reform* (Göteborg Studies in Educational Science 100). Göteborg: Acta Universitatis Gothoburgensis.

Carlgren, I. (1992). *På väg mot en enhetlig lärarutbildning? En studie av lärarutbildares föreställningar i ett reformskede* (Pedagogisk forskning i Uppsala 102). Uppsala: Uppsala Universitet, Pedagogiska Institutionen.

Cochran-Smith, M. (2003). Learning and unlearning: the education of teacher educators. *Teaching and Teacher Education 19*, 5–28.

De Fina, A. (2009). Narratives in interview—The case of accounts. For an interactional approach to narrative genres. *Narrative Inquiry 19*(2), 233–258.

Erixon Arreman, I. (2005). *Att rubba föreställningar och bryta traditioner. Forskningsutveckling, makt och förändring i svensk lärarutbildning.* Doktorsavhandlingar i Pedagogiskt arbete Nr 3. Umeå. Umeå universitet.

Freeman, M. (2006). Life 'on holiday'? In defense of big stories. *Narrative Inquiry 16*(1), 131–138.

Gee, J. P. 2001. Identity as an analytic lens for research in education. In W. G. Secada (Ed.) *Review of Research in Education, 25, 2000–2001*, 99–125. Washington, DC: American Educational Research Association.

Goodson, I. F., Biesta, G., Tedder, M., & Adair, N. (2010). *Narrative learning.* London and New York: Routledge.

Goodson, I. F. (1997). Representing teachers. *Teaching and Teacher Education 13*(1), 111–117.

Goodson, I. F., & Sikes, P (2001). *Doing life history in educational settings: learning from lives.* Buckingham: Open University Press.

Gov. Bill. (2009/10):89. *Bäst i klassen—en ny lärarutbildning.* [Best in class—a new teacher education]

Helsig, S. (2010). Big stories co-constructed. Incorporating micro-analytical interpretative procedures into biographic research. *Narrative Inquiry 20*(2), 274–295.

Jenkins, R. (2008). *Social identity. Third edition.* New York: Routledge.

Karlsson, M. (2006). *Livsberättelseintervjuer som socialt situerade handlingar [Life story interviwes as socially situated actions].* I H. Pérez Prieto (red.): Erfarenhet, berättelser och identitet. Livsberättelsestudier. Karlstad University Studies.

Karlsson, M., & A-C. Evaldsson. (2011). 'It was Emma's army who bullied that girl'. A narrative perspective on bullying and identity making in three girls' friendship groups. *Narrative Inquiry 21*(1), 24–43.

Lucius-Hoene, G., & Depperman, A. (2000). Narrative identity empiricised: A dialogical and positioning approach to autobiographical research interviews. *Narrative Inquiry 10*(1), 199–222.

Lunenberg, M., & Hamilton. M. L. (2008). Threading a golden chain: An attempt to find our identities as teacher educators. *Teacher Education Quarterly Winter*, 185–205.

Mills C. Wright (1959). *The sociological imagination.* New York: Oxford University Press.

Mishler, E. G. (1999). *Storylines: Craft artists' narratives of identity* Harvard University Press.

Murray, J., & Harrison, J. (2008). Editorial. *European Journal of Teacher Education, 31*(2), 109–115.

Pérez Prieto, H. (2008). *Ett liv i/med lärarutbildningen: Pensionerade lärarutbildares berättelser om sina erfarenheter av lärarutbildningen* [A life in/with teacher education: life stories of retired teacher educators]. Karlstad University, unpublished project description.

Rodgers, C. R., & Scott, K. H. (2008). The development of the personal self and professional identity in learning to teach. In M. Cochran-Smith, S. Feiman-Nemser and D.J. McIntyre (Eds.) *Handbook of research on Teacher Education. Enduring Questions in Changing Contexts, Third Edition*, 732–755. New York: Routledge.

SOU (1972) :26. *Förskolan.* (Del 1) Stockholm: Socialdepartementet.

SOU (1972) :27. *Förskolan.* (Del 2) Stockholm: Socialdepartementet.

Swennen, A., & Bates, T. (2010). The professional development of teacher educators. *Professional Development in Education 36*(1), 1–7.

Zeichner, K. (1999). The new scholarship in teacher education. *Educational Researcher 28*(4), 4–15.

AFFILIATIONS

Marie Karlsson
Karlstad University

Héctor Pérez Prieto
Karlstad University

BIOGRAPHIES

Avril Loveless is Professor of Education and Head of Research at the University of Brighton. Her research and teaching weave together three areas of theoretical and empirical work: understandings of creativity; pedagogy and teacher knowledge; and ICT capability within an early 21st century education system.

Carl Anders Säfström is Professor of Education at School of Education, Culture and Communication, Mälardalen University Sweden and Visiting Professor at Laboratory for Educational Theory at University of Stirling, UK.

Ciaran Sugrue is Professor of Education and Head of the School of Education, University College Dublin, Ireland. One of his most recent publications is Sugrue, C., & Dyrdal Solbrekke, T. (Eds.). (2011). *Professional Responsibility: New Horizons of Praxis*. London & New York: Routledge.

David Stephens is Professor of International Education at the University of Brighton. For the past thirty five years he has lectured and researched in a number of global Southern countries. He has published widely on issues of qualitative research, and in particular issues of culture in the carrying out of educational research. His latest book is *Qualitative Research in International Settings: A Practical Guide* (Routledge, 2010) which foregrounds context and setting in the research process. He is currently writing on Narrative in International Education and Development which will be published by Routledge.

Håkan Löfgren—Ph.D. in Educational Work at Karlstad University, Sweden. His research focuses on teachers' life stories and professional identity constructions in institutional settings.

Héctor Pérez Prieto is Professor in Educational Work at Karlstad University, Sweden. His current research interests include sociology of education, educational policy and narrative studies.

Ivor Goodson is Professor of Learning Theory at the University of Brighton. He has spent the last 30 years researching, thinking and writing about some of the key and enduring issues in education and. Life history and narrative research specialisations represent a particular area of competence as does research into teacher's lives and careers and teacher professionalism.

Maria Do Carmo Martin—Historian, Ph.D. in Education, Professor in the Department of Education, Knowledge, Language and Art, State University of Campinas (UNICAMP-Brazil) and Overseas Research Scholarship, funded by FAPESP in the Education Research Centre, University of Brighton (UK). Member of the 'Memory, History and Education' (UNICAMP) and at Network 'Education, Culture and Politics in Latin America'.

Marie Karlsson is Assistant Professor in Education at Karlstad University. Her research is mainly focused on life stories, narrative interaction and research interviews as social processes of identity making.

Molly Andrews is Professor of Sociology, and Co-director of the Centre for Narrative Research (www.uelac.uk/cnr/index.htm) at the University of East London, in London, England. Her most recent monograph is 'Shaping History: Narratives of Political Change'.

Pat Sikes is Professor of Qualitative Inquiry in the School of Education, University of Sheffield.

Pik Lin CHOI, an Assistant Professor at the Department of Education Policy and Leadership in the Hong Kong Institute of Education, researches primarily in teachers' lives, careers and gender identities.

Sheila Trahar is a Reader in the Graduate School of Education, University of Bristol. Her research reflects her commitment to inclusivity in higher education and she has published widely in the area of international higher education and intercultural learning and teaching. Her book *Developing Cultural Capability in International Higher Education: A Narrative Inquiry* was published by Routledge in 2010 and her edited collection for John Benjamins *Learning and Teaching Narrative Inquiry: Travelling in the Borderlands* was published in August 2011.

Ragna Ådlandsvik has been an Associate Professor in Teacher Education at the University of Bergen, Norway. Her research interests focus on learning through the life course, poetic language, and narrative learning.

CPSIA information can be obtained at www.ICGtesting.com
Printed in the USA
LVOW10s1017301013

359261LV00004B/142/P